Stop just getting through each d, impactful life God has called you to! *Finding the Extra in Ordinary* walks us through how to shake off the mundane and step into the truly extraordinary life Jesus wants us to experience. Buckle up and prepare for change!

CHASE HEADLEY, former Major League Baseball player for the New York Yankees and San Diego Padres

One of my greatest blessings is having Jeff Simmons as my pastor and friend and personally serving around the world with him through Justice & Mercy International. Jeff's faith and love for Christ are contagious. To read *Finding the Extra in Ordinary* is to be inspired by what God wants to do with your life. If you're wondering if your life has purpose or if God deeply loves you, pick up this book and be encouraged!

KELLY MINTER, Bible teacher and author of *The Blessed Life: A 90-Day Devotional through the Teachings and Miracles of Jesus*

You'll want to reexamine your life and priorities after reading *Finding the Extra in Ordinary*. God wants to do something extra in your life as you grow deeper in your relationship with Jesus. Jeff Simmons is an amazingly gifted pastor and teacher, and this book is an extraordinary example of those gifts.

BRETT JAMES, Grammy Award–winning songwriter and producer

Finding the Extra in Ordinary is a must-read for everyone searching for meaning in this life. So often we settle for an ordinary life when we know that God has more for us. This book offers the practical wisdom that leads to an extraordinary life. It calls us to a full and meaningful existence with a focus on what truly matters. Get ready to be challenged and inspired!

AMY ALEXANDER, marriage and family therapist and CEO and cofounder of The Refuge Center for Counseling

If you want to read about the power of a Spirit-led life written by someone who actually lives one, then this book, written by my dear friend Jeff Simmons, is for you. *Finding the Extra in Ordinary* is a reflection of how he lives what he preaches.

MIKE MINTER, founding pastor and pastor emeritus of Reston Bible Church

Everyday living can get to feeling downright ordinary. Ordinary breakfast with my ordinary coffee. Wearing my ordinary jeans to my ordinary job. Ordinary bills at the end of another ordinary day. Same old, same old. *Can God really use an ordinary person like me?* If you have forgotten what God loves to do with ordinary people, *Finding the Extra in Ordinary* offers just the inspiration you need. From the very first page, I was hooked by the amazing stories, biblical wisdom, and trademark joy of my friend Jeff Simmons. And by the end I realized, *God meant this book for me!*

ANGELA THOMAS PHARR, bestselling author and speaker

finding the extra in ordinary

finding the
EXTRA
in ORDIN-
ARY

EMBRACING THE BEAUTY
OF THE CHRISTIAN LIFE

JEFF SIMMONS

A Focus on the Family resource
published by Tyndale House Publishers

30	29	28	27	26	25	24
7	6	5	4	3	2	1

To God and to all those who long to pursue Him as they experience the extra in the ordinary.

contents

introduction

MOST PEOPLE SETTLE FOR ORDINARY. While almost everyone knows deep down there could be more to their life, they either don't know how to find it or they simply conform to what others are doing. So much in this world makes us feel ordinary, like a number or a statistic. Maybe you feel that way sometimes. Maybe you feel like just another number—your social security number, your driver's license number, your student ID number—but you are so much more. You were born for a reason.

For so many of us, life becomes monotonous. We wake up in the same bed, brush the same teeth, go to the same job, eat the same lunch, come home with the same fatigue, watch the same shows, fall asleep in the same bed, then wake up and do it all over again. Deep down we long for more. We long to be fulfilled and to make a difference. This longing needs to be expressed, heard, and met. When we finally stop for a moment and evaluate our lives, we can be honest about how we feel and what we really need. We can then determine to move beyond the ordinary.

What if, at this point in your life, everything could begin to make sense? What if you could understand and truly live life to the fullest? When you discover *why* you were created, it gives your life meaning. You move from living in the ordinary to embracing the *more* in life. It is powerful, freeing, and exhilarating. You immediately feel the difference, and it changes everything. No longer are you simply tired, worn out, and just trying to survive, but now you are energized, engaged, and fully alive. This is the life that only a few find. But for those who do find it, it changes everything. What if you could discover this way of living?

Let's be clear that we are not simply talking about behavior modification. Behavior modification is something we have all tried. Perhaps, for example, we want to lose weight. So we decide to try every weight loss plan out there. We modify our behavior to conform to some fad diet program. Sometimes we find success for a season, but for most of us, after a few months (or more likely days), we are right back where we were before. Life gets in the way and keeps us from our desired goal.

We need more than behavior modification to impact all areas of our lives. We need to dive into something deeper— something that impacts every area of life and is birthed from the inside out, not the outside in. Not simply behavior modification, but *life transformation*. This is where we truly come alive.

I met John several years ago. He was very successful by the world's standards. He had plenty of money, nice cars, and multiple homes. He had followed Christ for most of his life, but when he was in his midfifties, he experienced a defining moment. Everything changed when John embarked on a fishing trip in a remote location; that's when something new sparked in his heart. (I'll provide more details about John's trip later.)

It was like a light bulb came on inside him. From that moment forward, John completely embraced the life God had for him. He started to give back and invest in others. Joy filled his heart and life. Before this John had been very serious and intense, but afterward he became full of life, joy, and peace. One day he said, "I am in my fifties now. I just wish I had gotten it sooner. I feel so alive, but I wasted so many years."

At fifty-five, John finally began to live the life he was created to live. Maybe you, too, look back over your life and can see there were some "wasted years." You've most likely had some good years as well, but do you ever wonder if there is more to life? Something more that you were created to do or to be?

You are here for a reason. There is a reason you were born at this time in history. There is a reason you were born in the land of your origin. There is even a reason you were born into a particular family and community. There is a reason for your life, and finding that reason and the meaning behind it is crucial. It is worth your time, energy, and pursuit. It impacts everything.

An old quote sometimes attributed to Mark Twain says, "The two most important days in your life are the day you were born and the day you find out why." Throughout this book we'll explore *why* you were created and *how* to live it out. We'll explore God's plan for our lives and learn to see ourselves the way God sees us. I'll share stories of others who've chosen to follow God and to live their own extraordinary lives. And I pray that a light bulb will come on for all of us so that we might live whatever time we have left with meaning, purpose, and joy.

Most people decide to play it safe. In fact, most people live life afraid. Afraid to step out. Afraid to be bold. Afraid to discover why they were created. Afraid to know their reason and purpose. But there is so much more available! Don't we owe it to ourselves as well as to others to live the life God has planned for us? When we are willing to let go of what everyone else thinks and move past simply conforming to the world's standards, then we can move forward in discovering the life He wants for us.

As I look around, I see many wonderful people stuck on a journey of the ordinary. Some of them believe the lie they have been told all their life—that this is all there is; there isn't anything more. Others were told they wouldn't amount to much. And still others are living the life that someone else— maybe a parent, a significant other, a teacher, or a coach— planned for them, but it is not the life they want. So many people are gridlocked by fear and stuck in the ordinary or, sadly, the less-than-ordinary. But it doesn't have to be like this.

Many years ago, there was a group of ordinary guys. Some of them owned businesses, while others were working jobs just trying to make ends meet. Every day, they went to work to make enough money for their families to eat and have somewhere to live. Sounds like most of the world, doesn't it? They were good guys, even religious, but something was missing. Then one day, another man, who turned out to be God in human form, came along and invited them on a journey. He said, "Come, follow me" (Matthew 4:19, NIV). And their lives were forever changed.

They could have stuck it out with fishing or tax collecting, eventually dying in obscurity. But they traded the ordinary for following Jesus. And their lives, as well as our world, were never the same. For each of these disciples, there came a defining moment and then a daily commitment to the One who invited them to live beyond the ordinary.

I wrote this book because it is my desire to help people find their reason and purpose—to help them understand that they were designed by the Creator as unique, special, and in the image of God. I want others to understand that we were not born to be ordinary. Just like the men in the Bible whom Jesus called to be His disciples, for each of us there comes a defining moment and a daily commitment. The same call, the same invitation, that came to those guys back then still comes to us today.

Don't you desire more? I believe we all do. And this desire for more is part of our reason for being and our search for meaning. We were designed that way by God. We have been given one opportunity to live this life. One opportunity. There is no rehearsal. We won't get a mulligan or a do-over. This is it.

Live the life you were created to live. You have been given this one as a gift, and God has an awesome plan for you. Yes, *you*! And you have certain gifts, talents, and abilities to help you reach your potential in this life. I want you to reach your full potential, but even more so, God does too! Settling in life is why so many people never feel fulfilled, confident, or satisfied.

Maybe you have been there. You might feel tired, run down, even lost. Yet you don't have to live this way. God has the best life for you. Reading this book could be your defining moment—the point where you get serious about this invitation you have been given.

I've had the privilege of meeting a lot of incredible people, from celebrities here in the United States to precious orphan children around the world. I've met people of all ages and from all backgrounds and socioeconomic statuses, and I have made some remarkable discoveries along the way.

You'll meet many of these people in the pages that follow. They don't all look alike. They don't all sound alike. They don't all think alike. And no surprise, they don't all think exactly like me. They come from different places and have different points of view, but they all love God and have made a remarkable—dare I say extraordinary—difference for His Kingdom. I have gained new insights about life from every one of them.

I want to share these insights with you in this book because I am convinced that you can truly live a greater life. Don't settle for the mediocre, the mundane, or especially the ordinary. You can become all you were intended and created to be!

As long as you are alive, God is not finished with you. There is still breath in your lungs for a purpose. Think about this: "If God is for us, who can be against us?" (Romans 8:31). Seriously, the God of the universe is for you! And nothing His hands touch is simple or ordinary. Rather, what He creates is special and complex—from butterflies to beasts in the fields, from morning dew to thunderstorms that light up the sky. He created you, and He is for you. You get one shot at life—one chance—so don't waste it. Don't live for things that do not matter. Invest in what matters. Some of your best days are still ahead.

Let's jump in together with both feet. After all, what do you have to lose compared with what you have to gain—for His glory? As another famous quote—this one attributed to Theodor Geisel (famous children's author Dr. Seuss)—says, "Why fit in when you were born to stand out?" So stop fitting into the *ordinary* and start embracing the *extraordinary* life God created just for you.

1

the INVITATION

*It is not the years in your life but
the life in your years that count.*

ADLAI STEVENSON

IT WAS A NORMAL DAY at the office when my cell phone rang. A guy named Steve (he has a child who attended our church) was calling and said, "Jeff, you may remember me; I work with Dolly Parton. Dolly and Carl are celebrating their fiftieth wedding anniversary next weekend by renewing their wedding vows. Would you be able to officiate the service?" I told him that my work calendar was clear but I needed to check with my wife. I asked if I could call him back the following day.

When I came home and mentioned the call to my wife, Lisa, she flipped. "Dolly Parton! You are helping Dolly Parton renew her wedding vows?" Now, obviously, I knew who Dolly Parton was, but what I didn't know was just how much Dolly is loved worldwide. My wife was my first clue regarding the immense impact Dolly has had on so many people.

I learned quickly that almost everyone knows of Dolly Parton. She has a personality that draws people to her. Young and old, city people and country people, musicians and those who can't carry a tune—she has touched so many lives with her joy, her music, her humor, her love, and her generosity. She has captured the hearts of generations, especially here in Tennessee. As I look around my home state, I can see traces of Dolly everywhere. She's like the Tennessee rivers that help connect everything in the state.

Yet as famous as Dolly is, her family were "simple folk," as she would say. The fourth of twelve children, Dolly was born and raised in the hills of Tennessee—one of the poorest parts of the United States. But Dolly never really knew how poor her family was. She never complained about her circumstances but kept her head up and her heart focused on her dreams. Overcoming enormous obstacles at a young age, Dolly made it to Nashville and ultimately became the music superstar the world knows and loves today.

I called Steve back, and he gave me the details for the event. He told me that it would be held the next Saturday at a private location in Nashville. It would be a small, intimate ceremony, but there would be lots of pictures taken. Then he told me their story (and here is where I began to love Dolly like the rest of the world does).

Carl told Dolly that she could have anything she wanted for their fiftieth wedding anniversary. "Dolly," he said, "we can go anywhere in the world that you want. You say the word, and I will make it happen." Anything. Anywhere. Yet Dolly simply replied, "Well, Carl, here's what I want. I want a wedding dress, a wedding cake, a preacher, and us dressed up for lots of pictures. Then I want to sell the pictures and give all the money to the Imagination Library."

Here's a little background on all this. When Carl and Dolly were first married—fifty years earlier—Carl was twenty-three, and Dolly was twenty. Dolly already had a record deal in Nashville, and the record label did not want her getting married. So she and Carl slipped off to a little church in Ringgold, Georgia, for a small ceremony. Dolly wanted to get married in a church, and this little country church was the perfect place back then. Yet she always felt like she had missed out on a big, beautiful wedding.

Soon after they were married, Dolly won her first music award. Carl went with her to the elaborate awards ceremony, and after it was over, he told her, "Dolly, I don't ever want to do that again. That's you, but that's not me. You go pursue your dream. I will support you 100 percent, but that is not the life for me." From that point on, there have been no pictures of Carl at concerts or special events. None. How crazy is that! In a world filled with paparazzi, people have always wanted pictures of Carl. When Dolly was out on the road, Carl was busy doing work he loves back in Nashville. They are home and together often, and

Carl remains her biggest fan. They have been happily married all these years.

This brings us back to Dolly's wish for her vow-renewal celebration. She wanted them to dress up, say their vows before a preacher, take lots of pictures, and give all the money to the Imagination Library. If you aren't familiar with the Imagination Library program, Dolly's request will help you understand the heart behind the person.

Dolly knew that her home state was behind much of the country in terms of literacy, but instead of simply bemoaning the fact, she decided to do something about it. In honor of her daddy, Dolly created a book-gifting program that mails free, high-quality books to children from birth to age five, no matter their family's income. Books were initially distributed only to children in the county where she grew up, but the program became such a success that books were eventually distributed nationally and then internationally. Speaking from experience, I have three children, and our family received free books from the Imagination Library for all of them. Books are truly a life-impacting gift.

Dolly and her book-gifting organization have received honors and awards for their dedication to enriching the lives of children everywhere. It was another dream Dolly had that came to fruition and continues to grow. She's a small-town girl from one of the poorest areas in America, yet what a difference she is making!

When the day of their vow-renewal celebration arrived, my wife, Lisa, and I dressed up in nice clothes and drove to the special location. I had never before met Dolly or Carl, so I wasn't sure what to expect. Would I recognize her? Would there be security there to let us in? These thoughts ran through my mind as I pulled into the parking lot. As I got out of the car, I heard a voice with the most distinctive Southern drawl:

"Preeachhha!"

Dolly was standing there in a beautiful wedding dress. She walked over and threw her arms around my neck. "I'm so glad you are here! Come on in!" She introduced me to Carl— a sharp, good-looking, confident gentleman. Lisa and I were then introduced to Dolly's sisters and other family members. We also met her manager, the photography crew, and others. The multi-roomed venue was set up with a room for the ceremony, another room for the reception, which would feature a beautiful wedding cake, a room where the casual pictures would be taken, and a final room for the more formal photos.

Dolly was in top form. Her exuberance and beauty lit up the space. She was laughing and having the time of her life. As the photographers shot individual pictures of Dolly, Carl and I sat down to talk. He said, "Jeff, that is the most beautiful woman in the world right there." He went on to tell me how they had met and about their life together. Carl told story after story with a twinkle in his eye as he talked about his wife of fifty years.

"Jeff, she is also the most generous woman ever," he said. "She would give it all away if she could. She has put all her nieces and nephews through college. All that she does for everyone in East Tennessee, and then the Imagination Library—her heart is as big as this building. Sometimes I have to say, 'Hold on, Dolly! You can't just give it all away!'"

Then it was Carl's turn for individual pictures and Dolly's turn for stories. She talked about how people always wanted to see Carl. Since that first awards show, however, he has avoided the spotlight. She told me what a great husband he is, camera-shy or not. She talked about how supportive he is. She talked about when they met, and how much she still loves him. We talked about her family, her friends, and her faith. Dolly is truly everything people say she is—kind and authentic, full of life and joy.

It was time for more preceremony pictures, and Dolly informed me, "I'm going to make you famous, Preacher."

"I'm all good, Dolly," I replied. "You are famous enough for all of us." We laughed, posed, and simply had a great time together. Carl was engaged and willing to do whatever was asked of him. You could tell that he loved Dolly and that he was doing this for her.

We gathered on the platform for the renewal of the vows—only the preacher, bride, and groom, just like fifty years ago. It was a special moment. The love, the joy, and the commitment were all still evident.

Dolly Parton is anything but ordinary. She took what God gave her, didn't let poverty or the world stop her, and didn't settle for less. She dreams big. She loves generously. She is truly living her extraordinary life.

GOD USES REGULAR PEOPLE

God uses regular people. Sometimes we look at people in the world and think, *Well, they are just special* or *They have unique gifts and talents. They have something that I don't.* We look at many people in the Bible the same way. *They are supernatural. They have God-given gifts. They don't face the same struggles or have the same fears that I do.* Then we read stories of people who do incredible things and think, *They are sensational. They don't have my life.* Yet that is simply not true. Most of the figures in the Bible were just regular people, yet they didn't settle for the ordinary.

There are figures like Joshua, who was second-in-command to the great leader Moses. One day God told Joshua, "Moses my servant is dead" (Joshua 1:2). Maybe you have been there. The death of a parent. The death of a spouse or close friend. You are overwhelmed and wonder how in the world you will go on. Then God said to Joshua (just as He still says to us today), "Be strong and courageous! Do not tremble or be dismayed, for the LORD your God is with you wherever you go" (Joshua 1:9, NASB). Joshua, through the strength of the Lord, rose to the occasion and led God's people into the Promised Land.

Think of Mary, the mother of Jesus. When God was choosing an earthly mom for His Son, Jesus, you'd think He would have chosen someone well educated to teach His Son, someone wealthy to provide for Jesus, and someone well connected to help Jesus gain a following. Yet God chose a simple teenage girl—one from a small village and with little education. What set Mary apart was that she was honest, humble, and willing to be used by God. She trusted in God's sovereignty and accepted His call. God doesn't need our special abilities, just our hearts' availability.

Peter and John became leaders in the early church, and they impacted thousands for Jesus. Their influence continues today in churches throughout the world. One of my favorite verses in the Bible appears in Acts 4. In the previous chapter, Peter and John had healed a crippled man in the name of Jesus. In other words, a man who had been lame for more than forty years was now jumping around and praising God. The religious leaders arrested Peter and John because they were confused and couldn't figure out how they had done it. In truth, Peter and John had simply said, "In the name of Jesus . . ." as they told the man to rise up and walk. There is power in the name of Jesus.

Then comes this statement from Acts 4:13 regarding the religious leaders: "When they saw the boldness of Peter and John, and perceived that they were uneducated, common men, they were astonished. And they recognized that they had been with Jesus."

I love this! The religious leaders were dumbfounded! Peter and John were not seminary trained. They were not experts. They were unschooled, ordinary men. But they were bold, and the religious leaders realized that Peter and John had been with Jesus. When we are with Jesus, everything changes. We operate not in our own power but in the power of God. We are simply conduits for what He wants to do through us.

Peter and John were living their ordinary lives when Jesus called them to come follow Him. They began to grow in their faith and live for a greater purpose. They pursued the things of God more than the things of this world. For three years, they followed Jesus. (Some of you reading this have been following Jesus for a lot longer.) During that time, they were changed. Their hearts, minds, and desires were transformed. Jesus even told His disciples, "If you then, who are evil, know how to give good gifts to your children, how much more will the heavenly Father give the Holy Spirit to those who ask him!" (Luke 11:13). When you have a personal relationship with God through the grace and forgiveness of Jesus, God fills you with His Holy Spirit. The Holy Spirit fills every believer with God's comfort, wisdom, peace, and power.

Peter and John were ordinary until they were with Jesus, and then they were filled with the Holy Spirit. Jesus can do the same for all of us. You may think of yourself as ordinary, but through Jesus and the filling of the Holy Spirit, you are so much more. Think about this: The same power that raised Jesus from the dead is alive in you! The power and name by which Peter and John did miracles are the same power and name available to you today!

Peter and John saw God do a miracle through them. And this same God is still working wonders through His people. Some wonders are big, but many are small, day-to-day wonders wherein God intervenes on behalf of His people. Many people miss God working because they try to do it all on their own. They never stop to pray about a situation. They work to fix their problems first—to fix a relationship, to fix a struggle, to fix a fear—instead of praying and turning it all over to God.

This is where we move from ordinary to extraordinary: when we live a life of dependence on the Lord and invite Him into our everyday lives.

The world tells us to live for ourselves—to measure our lives by how much money we make, how much stuff we acquire, how many likes we rack up on social media. We look at others and think, *Wow, they are successful. They have a lot of money. They have a huge house or multiple houses. They have millions of followers on social media.* But God doesn't think like that. God is looking for people who are available to Him. It is not your ability but your *availability* that God is seeking.

Instead of making excuses, press into the Lord more. Truly love God, love others, and love yourself. Lean into the call He has on your life. No matter what stage of life you are in, you can still realize your God-given dreams and accomplish your God-given goals. All people are special and uniquely created and can be used by God—people in the Bible and people like you and me.

The Bible says, "For you formed my inward parts; you knitted me together in my mother's womb" (Psalm 139:13). Everyone in this world, everyone throughout history, has been created by God for a reason and a purpose. However, only a few ever figure that out. Only a few live the life that God called and intended them to live. These are the people we remember. These are the people who make a difference.

If you look back through history, it's often been individual Christ-followers living for God's agenda and not their own who have most impacted the world. It's been men and women who, instead of living for making the most money or having the biggest house or gaining the most followers, began to invest in God and His Kingdom. People who loved God and loved others. These are the people who have truly changed the world. Aren't you glad that Peter and John didn't spend their lives pursuing more money or bigger houses? They didn't settle for the ordinary life of the world.

Christ-following men and women throughout the ages have invested their lives in the things of God and not simply the things of this world. They've traded the temporary for the eternal. These Jesus-loving men and women have moved from ordinary lives to lives that truly make a difference for Jesus. After all, it was Christ-followers who started the first hospitals, orphanages, soup kitchens, churches, and more.

These men and women chose not to live for themselves but instead invested everything in ministries that would make a difference in the lives of others. What an impact! Our world has been transformed by hospitals, orphanages, churches, and more. People have received God's grace through these organizations and ministries. Many have seen the courage of these ordinary men and women and realized that these people have been with Jesus.

Can others see your courage? Do they see you not simply

living for the ordinary? Can they tell that you have been with Jesus? Choosing the eternal over the temporary isn't easy, but it is awesome. This is how you truly come alive through joy, peace, purpose, and adventure. You never know what God is going to do through you.

So begin waking up every morning and asking, "God, what do You want to do through me today?" This is exciting, and this is where you will see God do wonders. (We'll take a closer look at how God works a little later.)

DON'T DISQUALIFY YOURSELF

Moldova is one of the smallest and poorest countries in the former Soviet Union. It sits between Ukraine and Romania in Eastern Europe. There are many state-run orphanages in Moldova, and I have spent many years working with the precious children in these orphanages through the ministry of Justice & Mercy International. On my first few trips to Moldova, I met a young boy named Ilie. When I first met Ilie, he was about eleven years old. Ilie grew up in an orphanage without a mom or a dad. He had no money and nobody who cared deeply for him. Yet by God's grace, we were able to meet. Ilie didn't talk very much that first year, but I was able to share with him that God had a plan for his life.

Ilie is now in his early twenties and working with Justice & Mercy International, helping hundreds of orphan children in his own country. I asked Ilie a few years ago what had made the difference in his life. How did he overcome his obstacles and become such a great young man and a leader? Ilie replied, "You were the first person who ever told me that they believed in me. I realized I was loved and God did have a plan for my life."

God sent me halfway around the world to share this truth with this incredible young man. When Ilie began to understand that he was created for a reason and a purpose, his entire life changed. Since then, he's made a difference in many lives.

So many people disqualify themselves. They think, *I can't live an extraordinary life because I am just ordinary.* Ilie faced enormous challenges in his life, and he could have easily concluded that the challenges were too big to overcome. Dolly Parton could have concluded that since she was from such a small town and grew up poor, there was no way she could ever impact the world. Peter and John could have concluded that since they were just simple fishermen in a small, remote town, they were destined for an ordinary life. But don't ever forget about God's role. When you add God to the equation, everything changes. That is why I'm writing this book—I want to share this truth about God with you.

Here's what I have found about people who push beyond the ordinary: They focus on what they do have and not on what they don't. Many people spend their time focusing on what they don't have (*I don't have a lot of money. I don't have a lot of influence. I don't have a college degree. I don't have . . .*). They might spend hours scrolling through social media, looking at what everyone else has and feeling sorry for themselves. They watch others live the lives that they want to live.

It's easy to fall into the trap of "when and then" thinking: *When I get married or remarried, then I'll get serious about life. When the kids get out of school, then I will start living my best life. When the kids get into school, then I will have the time to invest in me.*

When I get more education.

When I get a raise.

When I get out of debt.

The list goes on and on (and so do the excuses!). But all this time is wasted in fixating on what you *don't* have instead of what you *do* have. Focusing on the problems allows people to naturally disqualify themselves from living their best lives right now.

People who are living their best lives right now don't spend time complaining about what they don't have. They don't wallow in the misery of things that haven't gone like they'd planned in life. Nobody has a perfect life—*nobody*. No celebrity in the world has it all together. Everyone is dealing with something. There's an old saying that goes, "Be kind, for everyone you meet is fighting a hard battle." It's true that everyone is fighting a battle of some sort, whether it's physical, mental, relational, financial, or something else.

No one has it all together, yet some people choose to push past the ordinary in spite of the challenges they face. These are the people who refuse to let the past or their troubles define who they are. They choose to find their hope and strength in Someone greater than themselves.

If you simply look to your own strength, then you will struggle. But there is Someone greater than all of us!

This world is not an accident, and neither are you. When you look at creation and see the intricacies of how everything fits together, are you filled with awe and wonder? Take a look around you—everything has a place and a purpose. The same is true of your life. You can spend your time focusing on what you don't have or on what has gone wrong, but when you realize there is a greater purpose to this life you are living, your entire perspective changes.

Everyone goes through struggles, but do you talk more about your struggles or more about your goals? Whether you were born with a lot or a little, you have enough to get started on this journey. You can't stay in the past. You can't let what you did *before* keep you from moving forward. Choose to see your past struggles as learning opportunities for the future.

I look back on my life and how wonderfully different it is from what I imagined it would be when I was a young boy or even a young man. How different it is from the script I had written for my life all those years ago. What's so different? The main thing is this—I let go and trusted God's plan for my life instead of my own. The more I sought God's greater purpose and His voice, the more He challenged me to step into the deep end of faith. The more I put my fear behind me, the more He was able to teach me and to use me. As I committed to Him daily, God reminded me that I was created to live beyond the normal. I can do anything in Christ because I serve a God of the impossible (see Philippians 4:13). By His grace, none of us were created to be ordinary.

As we are reminded in Isaiah 55:9, God has plans far greater than our own: "For as the heavens are higher than the earth, so are my ways higher than your ways and my thoughts than your thoughts." So often we think that an exciting and fulfilling life is something reserved for others. But God invites each of us into His greater story.

Of course, we can say *no* to God (and many people do). We can continue to live as we always have and continue to see the same results. We can choose to settle for our own little dreams. *Or* we can accept God's invitation and live the life that He has for us. It can all start today—right now. I challenge you to say *yes* and embark on this amazing journey. Move on from the ordinary and discover the extraordinary life God has for you.

It's time to let go of the past, embrace the joy of the future, and see the best in others and in yourself.

2

EMBRACE GOD'S HEART

Every man dies.
Not every man really lives.
WILLIAM WALLACE, *BRAVEHEART*

TWO OF MY FAVORITE PEOPLE in the world are Darrell and Connia. Darrell and Connia moved to Nashville from New York a few years ago after retiring from successful careers in the Big Apple. We met at church one Sunday and immediately connected. They had retired early and wanted, like many, to live closer to their grandchildren.

Darrell said that when he was growing up, his parents did not have a lot of money. He had to buy his own clothes for school. One year he only had money for a single pair of pants, a shirt, and some underwear. And when he got to the cash register, Darrell found that he didn't actually have enough money for all three items. His father said, "Well, you are going to have to put something back." This experience served Darrell well throughout his life, teaching him the importance of financial accountability and having a strong work ethic.

Connia's dad passed away when she was very young. Her mom raised her and her sister as a single parent while working multiple jobs. Connia's mom trusted God to do the impossible and taught Connia to do the same. Connia grew in her faith despite her family's challenges as she watched her mother take care of their family while still opening their home to others.

God was present in both of their lives, and they knew it. When Darrell and Connia met as young adults, they fell in love because they saw the heart of God in one another. Together they committed to putting God first in their marriage and promised to share God's abundant blessings with others.

Connia went on to become a senior executive in human resources for a large corporation in New York, and Darrell went to work, first as a police officer, then later as a senior corporate security agent. God blessed them with a wonderful daughter, son-in-law, and two grandsons. They are passionate about their family, serving God, and making a difference in the world. They are successful, godly, and living their best lives. They didn't settle or stagnate in life but have continued to grow, pursue God, and live the adventurous life that God has for them.

Have you ever thought, *Why was I born now—at this time*

in history? Or *Why was I born here—in this family, this city, this state, and this country?* You are not an accident. God, in His sovereignty, could have brought you into this world at any time in history and in any place. Yet He chose for you to be born here and now. If God is this specific, then don't you think He has a plan and a purpose for you? Of course He does!

Maybe you believe in God, or maybe you are not sure. But you do need to understand that there is more to this life than what you can see. And the first step to understanding this is aligning your life with the One who created this world and created you. The God of the universe has a great plan for His children (see Jeremiah 29:11)!

Begin by yielding your life to the One who created you and knows you by name. John 10:3 says, "The sheep hear his voice, and he calls his own sheep by name and leads them out." Then ask Him what He wants you to do with your life and what adventure He is calling you to. Why are you alive at this moment? The answer is simple: because God has a very intentional plan for your life.

This is the only way life makes sense. You can spend all your time trying to fix your circumstances. You can spend all your time trying to fix the people around you—your boss, your spouse, your boyfriend or girlfriend, your children, your friends. But until you settle the issue of your relationship with God, nothing else will fall into place. There will always be discontentment on the inside regardless of what is happening on the outside.

In his 1961 book *The Knowledge of the Holy*, author and pastor A. W. Tozer wrote, "What comes into our minds when we think about God is the most important thing about us." This is so true. If you believe that God is always mad at you or always out to punish you, then you will live a life of fear. You won't have any confidence in yourself. You won't believe you can accomplish anything great. But if you believe that God is *for* you, then you can live with confidence. You can view challenges as minor setbacks. You can know that God is with you and that He is for you.

Look at your life—what do you believe about God? Do you believe He is cheering you on, or do you feel He is mad at you because of your mistakes? Understanding the truth about who God is has the potential to change everything about how you live.

YOU ARE LOVED

You *are* loved! If you question this statement, then I encourage you to start spending time alone with the Lord and letting Him bring His Word to life in your heart. Consider again Psalm 139:13: "For you formed my inward parts; you knitted me together in my mother's womb." God handcrafted you, shaped you, and formed you before you ever came to be. You are not "one in a million"—you are one in about eight billion. There is no one in the world exactly like you. God created you, and you are beautiful. Believe anything less than this, and you are cheating yourself and those you could impact for His glory.

Maybe you grew up thinking God was always mad at you.

Maybe you attended a church that taught if you did anything wrong, God was waiting to zap you.

Or maybe you feel like God only loves you when you are good and when you do good.

But that is not who God is. God is for you. He loves you. Let's look at what His Word says:

- "Your steadfast love, O LORD, extends to the heavens, your faithfulness to the clouds" (Psalm 36:5).
- "God shows his love for us in that while we were still sinners, Christ died for us" (Romans 5:8).
- "In all these things we are more than conquerors through him who loved us. For I am sure that neither death nor life, nor angels nor rulers, nor things present nor things to come, nor powers, nor height nor depth, nor anything else in all creation, will be able to separate us from the love of God in Christ Jesus our Lord" (Romans 8:37-39).

Your life is not meaningless. When you know you are loved, you have the foundation to believe in yourself. Don't get distracted from the truth of what God says about you and why He brought you into this world. God has a purpose specifically for you.

On one of my early mission trips to Moldova, I met a young girl named Aliona. Like my friend Ilie, Aliona grew up in an orphanage without any parents. She spent every night sleeping two kids to a bed, with no one to read her a bedtime story, no one to tuck her in at night, and no one to help her during the day. Yet one summer, through one of our teams, she heard about this God of love and grace. Aliona committed her life to God and grew up knowing that He had a plan for her.

Aliona discovered that she was "fearfully and wonderfully made" (see Psalm 139:14). She heard from many of our teams that God had a unique plan for her life. Through her sponsor, she began to believe that what God said about her was true. While so many orphaned children end up being trafficked, living on the streets, or spending time in jail, there are a few who overcome the odds and succeed by the grace of God.

Today Aliona is a young adult and a wonderful leader. Like Ilie, she works for Justice & Mercy International, and she is returning to the orphanages she left behind in order to share the Good News of God's love. When asked for one word to describe her life, she replied, "One word would have to be that I am—what is the word?—*beloved*. Yes, I am beloved."

You are beloved too.

Darrell and Connia have achieved things by God's grace that they never knew were possible. Aliona also overcame enormous odds. So can you! Listen to God's truth about how much He loves you. Stay connected to the source, and watch Him move in your life.

YOU ARE BEAUTIFUL

The passage we read earlier in Psalm 139 continues, "I praise you, for I am fearfully and wonderfully made. Wonderful are your works; my soul knows it very well" (Psalm 139:14). We often look in the mirror and focus on our imperfections rather than being thankful for how God made us. When we are weak, we compare ourselves with photoshopped models or professional athletes until we are completely discouraged and overridden with envy. We listen to the lies of the enemy until we look nothing like Jesus!

But God made you, and He is pleased. It is written, "God saw everything that he had made, and behold, it was very good" (Genesis 1:31). Maybe you don't feel beautiful, but you are!

Developing a healthy view of yourself is key to living the life you were created to live. Do you spend more time living with a self-image or a God-image? Are you self-conscious or God-conscious? In 1 Samuel 16:7, God makes it clear: "Man looks on the outward appearance, but the LORD looks on the heart." Stop pursuing the affirmation of others, or what the world says you should be, and start listening to God. What does it say about us if we don't like our image even though God made us in His (see Genesis 1:27)?

So often we look at ourselves in a mirror and see everything that—at least in our minds—is wrong with us. Or we see ourselves in a photo and immediately wish we could change our looks. We think, *My nose is too big* or *I have too many wrinkles.* We struggle with our self-image because we compare ourselves with what our culture says we should look like (even though culture constantly changes). We put filters on our Instagram pics and selfies because "I don't like the way I look in that picture." We're convinced that we do not measure up, but who does?

This is not how God sees you. God doesn't see your imperfections; He sees someone created in His image. We are beautiful in God's eyes, but it's not a beauty based on our physical appearance. God looks at us and loves us. God loves *you.* You are special to Him. God created you, and He loves you just the way you are. God doesn't want you constantly comparing yourself with others; rather, He longs for you to embrace His heart for you. It's a game changer in life when you begin to embrace who you are in God's eyes.

GUARD YOUR HEART

There comes a point for each one of us when we have to decide what we believe about God. Is He truly good, and does He want the best for us, or not? The Bible shows us a God of love and grace, a God who does love us and has great plans for us. Will you believe this truth? Listen to this verse: "Above all else, guard your heart, for everything you do flows from it" (Proverbs 4:23, NIV). Protect your heart. Allow only the truth of what God says about you to enter in. This is how you overcome obstacles and keep going—and become even stronger.

We all go through challenging and difficult times, but all of us also experience good things. Let's not get tripped up on negative words spoken in the past. As much as they might hurt, let God remind you Whose you are and how special you are. Some people have the best intentions with their comments, yet these are often the most hurtful. Comments from those closest and dearest to us are hard to set aside. But don't let the past or anyone else define you and keep you down. Set your eyes on Jesus, and let Him define you through His Word.

Our challenge is that we have an enemy who doesn't want us to succeed. We think about the proverbial angel on one shoulder and devil on the other. The fact is that while God tells us who we are created to be, the devil (also known as "the father of lies") is frequently whispering deceit into our other ear.

While God says, "You are loved," the enemy says, "Who can love you?" The enemy works to point out all our flaws. The devil loves to remind us of our past mistakes. We feel the weight of shame and guilt pour over us. We remember when we messed up or when someone said something negative about us. The hurt and the pain are real.

The enemy specializes in shame and guilt. The devil constantly whispers to us, *You are not good enough. Remember what you did in high school or college?* He highlights our failures and shortcomings to make us feel worthless and discouraged. This is when the shame and guilt set in. This is when we hang our heads and go back to our same old lives. Shame is such a tool of the enemy.

In addition, the enemy tells us that we don't measure up. So many mothers carry "mom guilt"—the overwhelming feeling that they simply can't get everything done. Whether you're a mom who stays home with the kids, has a home business, or holds a job outside the home, there is always laundry and dinner and taking kids to places and longing to spend time with God and with family (and then there is more laundry). Mom guilt is very real, and it is not just women who struggle with the enemy's lies.

The enemy lobs many men bombs of guilt over jobs and careers. Are we earning enough money in our current jobs? Are we where we should be at this point in our careers? Are we keeping up with those around us regarding our homes, cars, lawns, and more? For dads who stay home with the kids while Mom works outside the home, the guilt can be just as stifling. And single parents have even more to handle! The enemy tries to keep us feeling guilty, whether for what we did in the past or for what we are not doing today. Of course we've all made mistakes, but our mistakes do not have to define us. We can be forgiven and redeemed!

LET GOD DEFINE YOU, NOT YOUR PAST

We all must determine if we will find our worth and value from the God of the universe or from the devil. As you evaluate where you are right now in your life, what do you believe? Do you believe God loves you and has great plans for you, or do you believe the lie that you are not good enough?

Here is what God says: "Remember not the former things, nor consider the things of old. Behold, I am doing a new thing; now it springs forth, do you not perceive it? I will make a way in the wilderness and rivers in the desert" (Isaiah 43:18-19). This is awesome! You don't have to live in the past. You don't have to be defined by your past. God is doing a new thing in your life.

When Jesus Christ died on the cross, He died for your past sins, your present sins, and your future sins. God redeemed you from your past. Psalm 103, beginning in the sixth verse, tells us that the Lord "works righteousness and justice for all who are oppressed." He "is merciful and gracious, slow to anger and abounding in steadfast love." God "does not deal with us according to our sins, nor repay us according to our iniquities." And, perhaps best of all, He has removed our sins far away from us—"as far as the east is from the west."

God has saved you for a reason. He has great plans for you! You can learn from your past, but you are not defined by it. You are defined by God and what He says about you.

GO FORWARD IN FORGIVENESS AND GRACE

There is a man in the Bible named David. He didn't grow up in a royal or wealthy family. In fact, he was the youngest of eight boys. He was essentially the runt of the litter. When his older brothers went off to war to fight for the kingdom, David stayed back to take care of the sheep. They all thought he was too young and too small to fight. But David developed a heart for God.

One day David went to take food to his brothers, who were fighting against a foreign army. When he arrived, a huge warrior from the opposing army named Goliath was taunting David's people and challenging anyone who was brave enough to come fight him. No one else took Goliath up on the challenge, so David stepped up and stepped out. Few could believe David was willing to do it, but all their negativity didn't stop him. David went out to battle Goliath "in the name of the LORD" (see 1 Samuel 17:45).

This became David's defining moment: when he trusted God and stepped out in faith. By God's grace, David won the battle. The other army was routed, and David became an overnight sensation. What followed was the hard part— not letting the success go to his head. Not finding his worth or value in money or prestige but keeping his heart pure toward God.

Through God's leading and grace, David went on to become king of the entire nation. He was incredibly successful. He led the nation well, and God blessed him with so much. However, one day David made a huge mistake. He took another man's wife into his bed. This was terrible enough, but instead of confessing his sin to God and working to make things right, David tried to cover it up. He arranged for the woman's husband to be killed in battle, then took her as one of his own wives. He thought he had gotten away with it, but God knew everything.

The enemy thought he had won, but David confessed his sin. And even though he came clean before God and his family, he experienced terrible consequences for his sin. This is the thing about sin—it often costs us more than we imagined. The enemy tells us, *It's no big deal. It doesn't matter.* There are almost always consequences, but when we confess, there is forgiveness and freedom.

The good news is that David didn't let his mistakes define him. He went on to become a more godly man, leader, husband, and father. David pushed past the ordinary and embraced the life God had for him. How many times must the enemy have come to David and whispered, *You are not good enough. Don't you remember what you did?* And how many times did David have to respond, "Get behind me, devil. I am forgiven and redeemed"? Yes, there were consequences for David's sin, yet David still had his best life ahead of him. At the end of David's life, he was known as a man after God's own heart (see Acts 13:22).

We will all make mistakes. There will be times when we feel like we don't measure up. But don't forget about the goodness and grace of God. Don't forget Who defines you. God is with you, and He is for you. Will you trust Him? Maybe you need to ask for forgiveness for something in your life. Don't wait; do it now. Don't make excuses. Afterward, move forward in the forgiveness and grace that God gives you. Don't dwell on your mistakes; think about the goodness of God. Don't think about how God can't use you; instead, focus on how God has called you "for such a time as this" (see Esther 4:14).

BE WILLING TO ADAPT TO GOD'S PLAN FOR YOUR LIFE

I recently had dinner with Tim Tebow. If you aren't familiar with Tim Tebow, then just know this—he is big, strong, and passionate about his faith in Jesus. Tim was a Heisman Trophy winner at the University of Florida. He went on to play quarterback in the NFL. He even won a playoff game for the Denver Broncos. After his football career ended, Tim decided to try professional baseball. He is an incredible athlete, but what makes Tim extraordinary is his commitment to Jesus. As anyone who knows him will attest, Tim lives out his faith.

When we were at dinner, Tim was telling me about his work with the Tim Tebow Foundation. What they do around the world is incredible. When Russia invaded Ukraine in 2022, Tim and his foundation immediately helped activate ministry connections to assist orphans, people with special needs, and families in crisis. Through some of their participating Night to Shine churches and other official ministry partners, the foundation was able to impact many in need, as well as help with evacuations and set up an integration center in a neighboring country. As I listened to Tim describe their efforts, I was engaged by his willingness to do whatever it takes to help some of the world's most vulnerable people.

Maybe you can't start a foundation or help thousands of children, but each of us can help one person. What makes a person extraordinary is not being able to throw a football or hit a baseball—there are people all over the world who can do that to some degree. But when you help someone who can't do anything for you in return? That is next level. Lots of ordinary people think about how much fame, money, and popularity they can secure for themselves. This is their common goal—more wealth, more success, more recognition. This line of thinking is shallow and short-lived, yet it is why so few ever experience impact, depth, joy, and true purpose. But as Tim's life demonstrates, God has so much more for all of us.

Tim posted these words to Instagram on May 7, 2022: "The purpose of life is not to be happy. It's to love God and to love people, to be of service, to be compassionate, loving, honorable, to have it make some difference that you have lived and lived with significance."

After our dinner that night, Tim spoke to an arena full of men at our Versus Men's Conference in Nashville. Tim told stories about men being bold for the Lord and living their lives with a different purpose. After he spoke, he invited men who wanted to follow Jesus with their lives to come down and take a stand in front of the thousands who had gathered. That night more than forty men came forward. Men who were committing to live their lives for Jesus, perhaps for the first time. These men were moving beyond the ordinary to begin living an extraordinary life.

Maybe you would never feel comfortable speaking to an arena full of people, but you could invite a friend or a family member out for coffee and talk to them about what God is doing in your life or theirs. You can pray for someone. You can reach out to someone and challenge them not to settle for the mundane things of this world but to know the One who calls us to the adventure of a lifetime.

LET THE ADVENTURE BEGIN

There is an old Chinese proverb that says, "A journey of a thousand miles begins with a single step." God is inviting each of us on the adventure of a lifetime. Remember, when Jesus called His first disciples in Matthew 4:19, He said, "Follow me." He did not say where He was leading them or how long they would be gone. He did not give them a list of what to bring. He simply called them to follow Him. It's all about beginning a relationship with God through Jesus Christ. This is where the adventure begins, and it's one that continues for a lifetime.

Can you imagine those first disciples? They had no idea what Jesus was calling them to. They had no idea of the miracles they would see or the joy they would experience. They had no idea of the lives they would watch be transformed or how their obedience would impact human history. They could never dream of seeing Jesus being crucified on a cross, conquering death, and being resurrected. They could never imagine watching Jesus ascend into heaven and experiencing the power of the Holy Spirit come upon them. They could never fathom the founding of the Christian church and how they would become leaders in this history-altering, eternity-impacting, life-changing movement of God. They had no idea. All they knew was to follow—to trust Jesus and to take a step of faith.

God doesn't tell us all the great things He wants to do in and through our lives when we start the journey—and if He did, we would probably never believe Him in the first place. So He just invites us to follow. To step out. To trust. This is where the adventure begins. And the best is yet to come. This is what I love about following Jesus. Every day I wake up and wonder, *God, what are You going to do today?*

What next step in your spiritual journey is Jesus calling you to take?

Maybe it is accepting Christ as your Lord and Savior. Perhaps you have been around church and religion your entire life, but you have never fully committed your life to Him. Why not today?

Maybe it is being baptized. Jesus was baptized at the age of thirty, and this is when He formally began His earthly ministry. If you were baptized as an infant, that is great, but that was really your parents' decision, not yours. There might come a time when, as an adult, you decide to be baptized in order to publicly demonstrate that you have fully committed your life to Jesus. Jesus was and is fully God, but He was baptized to set an example for us. It's remarkable that it was at Jesus' baptism when God sent the Holy Spirit and spoke over Jesus: "And behold, a voice from heaven said, 'This is my beloved Son, with whom I am well pleased'" (Matthew 3:17).

Maybe your next step is to pour into your family spiritually, to pray for your spouse and to make disciples of your children. If you are single, then your next step might be to invest in godly relationships.

Maybe it is going to a local church consistently and uniting with other Christ-followers. Maybe it is starting to read your Bible every day—learning what God is saying to you. Maybe it is beginning to pray, setting aside ten, fifteen, or thirty minutes every day to speak with and listen to God. (We will explore this more in the next chapter.) Maybe it is joining a small group at your local church. Maybe it is journaling—writing down your thoughts and prayers to God. Maybe it is going to a pastor or a Christian counselor and finding some help for an area of sin or struggle. Maybe it is serving at church. Maybe it is starting a Bible study at school or at work. Maybe it is going on a mission trip or sponsoring an orphan. Maybe it is helping build God's church.

I don't know what it is for you, but I know we can all take a "next step" on this adventure.

Jesus is inviting each of us to follow Him. It is not about the outcome, but about obedience. We all have a next step to take in life, and I pray that through this book and the Spirit of God, you will be challenged to move forward with Jesus. Your best days are still ahead. Let's go!

3
LISTEN

*If you think you can
or you think you can't,
you are right.*
ATTRIBUTED TO HENRY FORD

GRADUATING FROM COLLEGE was a stressful time for me. I was praying and asking God what I was supposed to do with my life. My degree was in finance and marketing, since I had always wanted to have a career in business. My dad had been in business, and I thought this was the direction for my life as well. I knew many well-respected people in business who were successful. I wanted to be a godly businessman, be involved in a church, make money, be generous, go on mission trips, and be active in my community. I still have plenty of respect for Christian businessmen and women, yet I had an unsettling feeling in my soul when it came to this career path. I didn't know what was causing this, but I could not find the peace in my heart that this was where I should be.

I was interviewing for a job one day, and I was convinced that this job was *the one*. The salary was great, and the company was strong. That night, however, I could not sleep. I kept tossing and turning. (Have you ever been there?) Finally I slid out of bed and down to the floor. I prayed, *God, if this is You, then speak to me. I will listen.* I can't explain it, but inside I felt there was this still, small voice speaking to me. I truly felt like God was saying, *This is not it. Trust Me. I have called you into ministry.*

I remember thinking, *What? Ministry?* Throughout the rest of that night, I wrestled with God. Everything in me thought my future was in business—the familiar, the money, the success—but I knew that God was specifically calling me to something different. At the end of the night, I thought, *Okay, God. If this is what You are calling me to, then I will follow. I don't know how it will go, but I will trust You.* There were way more questions than answers in that moment, but I knew God was speaking to me, and I wanted to follow Him.

The next day I thanked the company for their time but told them I was headed in a different direction. They were kind, and we left on good terms. Not long after this, a church called and asked me to come meet with them about leading their ministry to middle school, high school, and college students. The first night I served there, I knew this was where I would thrive. It was incredibly fulfilling to be with these students and watch God work in their lives. From this experience God led me to attend seminary, to plant a church, and ultimately to launch a nonprofit organization. I was now a part of what only God could do. I would never have dreamed of all God had in store for me.

I truly believe that God wants to speak to and lead each one of us. How will you respond? Will you hold on to the familiar, the ordinary? Or will you trust God and follow Him? Whether you are in business, a teacher, a student, a parent, or in ministry, God has a plan for you. God doesn't typically reveal all He will do; He simply invites us to trust Him. We learned in the last chapter that the most important thing isn't the outcome (or success); it's obedience. As we follow God, lives are impacted and His Kingdom grows.

WHO ARE YOU LISTENING TO?

So often we try to find the plan for our lives based on those around us. We listen to what others say about us or the way the world defines us. We try to measure up to other people's standards. We even look at people we think are successful in this world and then model our lives after theirs. We believe that God has a specific plan for us, yet we spend much of our time looking at social media and determining what we believe about ourselves by trying to figure out what others see in us. But what if we could start with God and listen only to what God says about us?

Who are you listening to? Are you listening to the God who made you and to those who have godly wisdom, or are you listening to those who settle for the ordinary? Other people may not have the best advice for you, but the One who created you always does. Pursue God, read His Word, and surround yourself with godly people. As the saying goes, you become like the company you keep. First Corinthians 15:33 puts it plainly: "Do not be deceived: 'Bad company ruins good morals.'" It's a good idea to ask yourself, *Are the people around me making me better or bitter?*

We have an enemy who will whisper in our ears, *God can't use you. You are just an ordinary person.* But God chooses ordinary people. After all, if God uses regular people to accomplish His purposes, then He is the One who receives the glory. What happens then is that people won't say, "Wow, *you* are so awesome!" Instead they will say, "Wow, *God* is so awesome!" That is the goal, isn't it—to bring glory to God?

Perhaps the enemy might whisper in your ear, *How can God use you? Think about all the mistakes you've made!* But this is when we respond, *Get out of here, devil! My God is greater! My God is a forgiving God, and I am redeemed in Christ. God has removed my sins as far as the east is from the west. He made me a new creation. I am fully His.*

When the enemy speaks lies to you or tries to cause doubt, speak Scripture back to him like Jesus did. Stand firm, speak the truth, and give God the glory. Ephesians 2:10 says that "we are his workmanship." Imagine—you were handcrafted with infinite skill and artistry! If God says you are His own masterpiece, then you should believe nothing less.

Are you listening to the One who created you, or are you

listening to what others say about you? Those around you might try to keep you feeling ordinary. We all have to deal with our own hidden motives, so be careful of the motives of others. Family members and close friends will want the best for you; they sincerely want you to reach your full potential. But there are always those who don't really know what is best for you. They might speak loudly, but you must listen instead to the One who speaks to your heart.

So many times we turn to social media to figure out what others think of us. We look at others and think we don't measure up. Yet we typically see only their highlights, because most of us post only our best moments. Thus we compare our worst moments or our mistakes with other people's best moments. Or we compare ourselves with celebrities and models who have been airbrushed to perfection. We can never look like them because what they show us is deceiving.

We can't rely on the impractical, unrealistic voices that shout at us through culture and social media. The ones who don't see our potential or worth. The ones who often don't want us to succeed. No, we must stay attentive to the voice of the One who created us. The One who consistently affirms, encourages, and loves us. The One who protects us and shields us. The One who is both with us and for us.

I'm probably not the best person to consult regarding a potential career in music—I have no musical talent, though I do love to sing in church!—but on the subject of knowing God and following His plan, I have worked with thousands of people and observed many more. Here's what I know: God created you, and He loves you. If you truly commit your life to Him through His Son, Jesus Christ, He will guide you and lead you. God wants you to reach your full potential in Him, and He will bless your life beyond what you could ever dream.

In the story we looked at in Acts 4, Peter and John were eventually brought before the religious leaders of the day. (These were the same people who had Jesus put to death, but Jesus conquered the grave and made a way for all of us.)

These religious leaders were still upset that Peter and John had healed the lame man "in the name of Jesus." So they called for the two men and commanded them to stop speaking or teaching in His name. I can't tell you how much I love Peter and John's reply. They said, "Which is right in God's eyes: to listen to you, or to him?" (Acts 4:19, NIV). Isn't this awesome? Peter and John determined that they were going to listen to God regardless of what anyone else said.

Have you resolved to do the same in your life? The world will tell you that you can't do something. The world will tell you that you don't measure up. The world will tell you to not even try. I mean, ordinary is good enough for most people, so why do you want to be different? Why would you desire to live for more?

Because you have determined to listen to what God says, and not anyone else.

God's plan for your life is extraordinary. Peter and John chose extraordinary living. They could have stayed content as fishermen, but they followed Jesus and were used to help change the world. They followed Jesus and saw miracles unfold before their eyes. Can you imagine seeing Jesus give sight to a blind man? Or tell a lame man to get up and walk? Can you imagine being there when Jesus said, "Lazarus, come forth!" to a man who had been dead for four days— and watching that same man come walking out of the tomb? (By the way, it's a good thing that Jesus spoke this man's name alone, or a whole bunch of formerly dead people might have come walking out!)

Peter and John committed their lives to following Jesus, and they had a front row seat to see Him change the world. Don't settle. Embrace the life God has invited you to live. And then watch Him do wonders in you and through you. Life becomes exciting when you listen to God! Your best days are still ahead.

So what keeps us from listening to God? Well, for one thing, we are usually busy listening to the world. We have so much noise in our lives that we can't hear God. There are so many voices calling out to us. We get in our cars and turn on music right away. Social media constantly invites us to scroll through, watch, and listen. Then there is the news, along with movies, TV, and streaming stations. Add to this list employers, teachers, coaches, family, friends, and crying babies. We can't even hear ourselves think.

In Psalm 46:10, God says, "Be still, and know that I am God." It is so hard for us to be still. We are always moving and going. Yet when we go on a vacation to the mountains or the beach, we feel so much more invigorated and rejuvenated.

When we can find time to go for a walk or sit in a chair, we usually feel more inner peace. Are you able to listen? Begin praying, "God, what do You want to say to me?" And then listen. God will speak. Not audibly, for the most part, but He will speak in His still, small voice to your heart.

God still leads His people today. Many times we want a "burning bush," like the way God spoke to Moses in the wilderness. I have found that God doesn't do that today, but there are four primary ways in which I believe God does speak to His people today.

God speaks through His Word—the Bible. God spoke to Moses through a burning bush because Moses didn't have the Bible. For that matter, none of the people mentioned *in* the Bible actually had the entire Bible to read and reference! Now we have God's complete Word in our hands and on our phones. The challenge, however, is that—at least much of the time—we don't read it. We don't take the time to dive into God's Word.

We want to know what God wants us to do, but we are busy trying to figure it out on our own. Many times God uses His Word to speak to our hearts. There are times when we read a passage in the Bible and think, *That is just for me!* God speaks through His Word to nourish our souls and to help guide our steps. God wants to direct us.

God's Word is also a great "guardrail" for us. God will not call us to do something that contradicts His Word. If you have an idea for your life, or if someone else is directing you, but it doesn't line up with what God's Word says, then it is not from God. If someone says you should cheat on your taxes, compromise your marriage, or even buy something for which you don't have the money, then you should know right away that you are listening not to the voice of God but rather to the lies of the enemy. Be wise and discerning. God's Word gives you parameters for decision-making and truths on which to build your life.

God speaks through godly people. Just as God did in Bible times when He raised up prophets and apostles to speak to His people, so God still speaks through others today. There might be times when you are sitting in a church service and feel like you are the only person in the room. It is as if the speaker is talking directly to you. That is the power of the Holy Spirit. God sometimes speaks through pastors in church, but He can also speak through other Christ-followers.

If you have godly parents, be grateful, for that is such a gift! Try to listen to what they tell you. Many times children assume that their parents don't know anything. But as we get older, we start to realize, *Hey, wait a minute, my parents are really pretty wise after all!* God can speak through parents, grandparents, and other family members. You are a member of your family for a reason.

If the rest of your family are not Christ-followers, God can still put other wise people in your life, such as small group or Bible study leaders, teachers, coaches, and friends. If we pay attention, then much like God spoke through Moses, David, and the other biblical prophets, God can speak to us through others. Maybe you're facing a tough decision and you really want to know God's will for you. Ask someone you trust for godly advice and for prayer. It is amazing how God can speak through the people around you.

God speaks through "God-incidences." I don't believe in coincidences, but I do believe in God-incidences. There might be times when you are praying about a decision regarding a job or a relationship. Then, as you pray, God might open or close a door. This is often a way that God makes His will and His way clear to you.

Perhaps a job offer comes "out of nowhere." It could be that God is opening a door. Or someone comes into your life whom you can help. Or maybe there is a small group or other ministry at church that aligns just right with your schedule. Don't look at these events as mere coincidences; look at how God might be speaking to you in these moments.

You can still say *no* to God and walk away. Many people do that. Many people do their own thing and wonder why God doesn't direct them. But if we begin looking at our circumstances with spiritual eyes, we will be able to see that God is speaking to us more than we realized. What if every day we woke up and said, "God, speak to me today and use me for Your glory"? Don't you think we would begin to look at daily scenarios a little differently? God wants to speak to you daily.

God speaks through His "still, small voice." (First Kings 19:12 also refers to God's voice as "a low whisper.") As mentioned earlier, we need to be still so that we can hear what God is saying to us. Find time each day to pray and/

or meditate. We often think of prayer as us talking to God. Much of the time those prayers sound more like "Help me, God!" We usually pray when we are in trouble. We don't have a way out, so we call out to God.

Yet prayer is not only talking; it is also listening. Prayer is a two-way conversation. If you have friends who talk all the time, you probably don't want to hang out with them for long periods of time. God gave us two ears and only one mouth for a reason, and learning to listen to God is essential to growing in your spiritual life. Carve out time each day to pray—to present your requests to God, but also to listen to His still, small voice.

GOD THE FATHER

Here's the greatest news of all (yes, I've said this before, but it's extremely important): You are loved. If you have committed your life to Jesus, then you are a child of God with a devoted heavenly Father. You are not a spiritual orphan. Remember, we all need someone to believe in us, and you have that.

What remains consistent when we move from the Old Testament to the New Testament is the concept of our covenant with God. *Testament* literally means *covenant*. Thus we proceed from the Old Covenant to the New Covenant. The Old Covenant was about God's law—the Lord revealing His character of righteousness and showing His people their need for a Savior. The New Covenant is one of grace—God revealing His Son and demonstrating sacrificial love for His people. God's grace is a game changer, yet many people live like God is always mad at them. They think that when they sin or mess up, God is waiting to punish them. That's why the concept of grace seems so radical.

Enter Jesus Christ. Jesus came along at the beginning of the New Testament and told the people to call God "Father." This teaching was incredibly radical at the time. Most of God's followers had extreme awe and reverence for Him, but they weren't all ready for the concept of a personal relationship with God as Father.

Then Jesus showed up on the scene. In the earliest days of His ministry, He said, "When you pray, go into your room, close the door and pray to your Father, who is unseen" (Matthew 6:6, NIV). What? Jesus just said to pray to our "Father"? This was different. Jesus went on to teach the most famous prayer of all, the "Lord's Prayer"—also known as the "Our Father" (Matthew 6:9-13). Jesus instructing His followers to call God "Father" was definitely radical—far more radical than we can even imagine. The sovereign God of the universe wanted us to have a relationship with Him and to know Him as intimately as a child knows their parent.

Some people struggle to accept God as Father because they had a terrible earthly father. If this describes you, I want to let you know I am so sorry for that. I have seen the impact of father wounds countless times. I know people who still live for their dad's approval even though their earthly father has been dead for years. Please, please don't project those flawed impressions onto God. Earthly fathers are human and make a lot of mistakes. But God is your heavenly Father, and He is perfect. He will still be there for you when everyone else is gone. You can find your true worth and value in what your heavenly Father says about you.

My wife, Lisa, did not have a great dad growing up. He never told her that he loved her. This is heartbreaking to me and something she still struggles with today. But she has also learned to find her worth and value in her heavenly Father, and it's made all the difference in her life.

(An important side note for all of us: Whether or not you had loving parents, you need to tell the people around you that you love them. Tell your spouse, your children, your friends, and all those you are close to. Words have power, so say them out loud. The words *I love you* are not simply assumed. The people you love need to hear you say them. Often. One of my goals is to tell my wife and kids that I love them every single day of my life. We all need to hear those words.)

People often wonder, *Why do bad things happen to good people?* Maybe you have contemplated this question in your own life. The fact is that we live in a broken and fallen world. In the beginning, God created a perfect world. Everything was great, at least for the first two chapters of the Bible. Adam and Eve were in right relationships with God and with each other. They knew God and each other intimately.

But then they sinned. They decided that they didn't want

to do things God's way. They sinned first, and the rest of us have been repeating that mistake ever since.

The truth is that hurting people hurt other people. It was true once Adam and Eve sinned, and it's still true today. One day Jesus will come back and make all things right, but until then the better question is *Why is there any good in the world today?* I mean, nobody is good on their own merit. We are all sinful, craving our own way and our own desires. The only reason there is any good in the world is because of God.

This is what God did for us: "For God so loved the world that he gave his one and only Son, that whoever believes in him shall not perish but have eternal life" (John 3:16, NIV). God gave His only Son out of love. He sent Jesus as a sacrifice for our sins so that we could be forgiven and restored. God loves His creation so much that those of us who believe in Him are called "children of God" (1 John 3:1, NIV). How amazing is it that God invites *us* into His family? We are no longer spiritual orphans, but are loved, redeemed, and restored.

When we have a relationship with God through His Son, Jesus, our call becomes to love like Him. "Dear friends, let us love one another, for love comes from God. Everyone who loves has been born of God and knows God. Whoever does not love does not know God, because God is love" (1 John 4:7-8, NIV). Yes, God *is* love. It is His nature, His character. The only reason we even have love in the world is because of God and His people. Therefore, we must be the ones to live it out. Where else will people find love in this world? Social media? Politics? School? Work? Business? None of these offer true, selfless love.

Since God is love already, there is nothing you can do to make God love you any more than He already does, and there is nothing you can do to make God love you any less. When we learn this, believe this, and live this, it changes everything. We never have to worry about doing something so bad that we might lose God's love. We can get off the roller coaster of performance anxiety and rest in His perfect love and grace toward us.

I have a good friend who grew up without an earthly father. Brandon was raised by a single mom who did a great job pouring love into him, but he always longed for a dad. He longed to know the love of a father.

Enter God.

As a teenager, Brandon was invited to church, and there he committed his life to Christ. In God, he found the love of a father that he so desired and craved. God met his deepest needs. Instead of remaining bitter and angry that his earthly father had walked out on him and his mother, Brandon experienced life-changing freedom.

He is now full of God's presence. He's found his worth and value in who God says he is. Brandon has been, and continues to be, a great earthly father to his own children and grandchildren. He has influenced many lives for the better thanks to God's grace and knowing God as his Father. He has transformed his family and impacted multiple generations simply by living to please his heavenly Father.

As we've learned, Jesus teaching us to call God "Father" was a radical new way of thinking. After all, the job of a father is to provide for, protect, and love his kids. This is what God does for us. So why worry? Our heavenly Father has us covered. Why be afraid? Our heavenly Father is greater than anything we face on earth. Why seek acceptance from others? Our heavenly Father knows what we need to feel accepted and whole. He is always there for us. In Him, we can rest assured that we are fully accepted and fully loved. We can pour into and impact others for good when we have confidence in God as our Father.

WHO ARE YOU FOLLOWING?

When I was growing up, the kids in my neighborhood liked to play follow-the-leader. It was a lot of fun, as the leader would make us do crazy things. We climbed over rocks, jumped out of trees, and ran through water. We laughed and enjoyed the game. No one (for the most part) got hurt, and there were virtually no long-term consequences. Yet as we grow up, we need to be careful who we follow because there *are* potential long-term consequences. What's more, when *we* become the leaders, we need to be careful and lead well when others follow us.

The apostle Paul wrote, "Follow my example, as I follow the example of Christ" (1 Corinthians 11:1, NIV). This is a bold statement, at least in my opinion. Why? Well, we should first examine our lives to see who we are following.

Whether it is a political leader, a spiritual leader, or a social media influencer, we all have people we follow in one way or another. We need to be sure that those we follow demonstrate godly character and integrity. No one is perfect, but are the people we follow leading us closer to Jesus or further away? There are definitely long-term consequences in this version of follow-the-leader—both for us and for generations to come.

As a pastor, I meet with a lot of people for counseling, both formally and informally. I often hear "Well, I had these friends . . ." When people tell me about some bad decision they made, some trouble they got into, that's when these so-called friends inevitably make an appearance. The people around us have a big influence on our lives, which explains why we so often become like the company we keep.

I remember meeting with a man who had had an affair. He was heartbroken. His actions almost destroyed his family. "I was out with these friends," he told me, "and they dared me to hit on this girl. I did it, and she responded. And my life has never been the same." Who are you listening to? If the people you hang out with are not a good influence, then it's time to change your friends. Seriously, find different friends, find a different job. Be around people who help make you a better person, not someone worse.

What also makes Paul's statement bold is that at some point in our lives, most of us will act as the leader. Leadership is a gift. Paul knew it, and he lived it. I love how he said, "Follow my example"—and didn't end there. Paul was not simply trying to amass more followers for himself. He said, "Follow my example, *as I follow the example of Christ.*" His goal was to lead others to Jesus. We have much the same goal—to point others to Jesus. It's our task to speak words of blessing and encouragement into other people's lives.

Paul could tell others to follow his example because he followed Christ's. Can you say the same thing? Are you following Christ's example? Are you passionate about directing those you influence toward the ultimate Leader? If you pursue and prioritize Jesus in your own life, then your actions will likely influence those who follow you. It will become natural. Paul was so passionate about Jesus that he basically told everyone, "Come on, guys—follow me, 'cause I'm following Jesus." It's on us to demonstrate with our words and our actions that we follow Jesus.

Leadership is a form of influence, so use your influence for the glory of God. Talk to your "followers" about Jesus. Maybe that's just your family members, but it's a start. Pray with your children. Bring your family and friends to church. Post some Scripture on social media. Use the influence you've been given to help make an impact that will outlast you. Speak words of hope and life into those around you. It *does* matter.

Here's what's so awesome—yes, I'm saying it again: God loves you, and He wants you to know it. Will you listen to Him? Will you listen when He says that He loves you "with an everlasting love" (Jeremiah 31:3)? Will you listen when He says that nothing can separate you from the love of God (see Romans 8:38-39)? Will you listen when His Word says, "See what kind of love the Father has given to us, that we should be called children of God" (1 John 3:1)?

Listen to your heavenly Father's voice. Listen to His plan for your life. Don't listen to the world, the culture, or your "friends" who are far from God. Who you listen to and what they say is essential to you moving beyond the ordinary.

4

MAKE the MOST of YOUR LiFE

*The measure of a life,
after all, is not its duration, but its donation.*

PETER MARSHALL

I WAS RECENTLY PART OF A FUNERAL for a young adult who had attended our church. Funerals are never easy, but they're especially tough when the individual who passed was only twenty-one years old. Krystal Adams was an amazing young lady who was a big part of our church family. When Krystal and her parents first visited Rolling Hills Community Church, Krystal had already been battling brain cancer for five years and was confined to a wheelchair. It didn't take long to realize there was something special about her.

Along with her father, James, Krystal committed her life to Christ. I will never forget the Easter Sunday morning in 2018 when they were baptized together. James said it was the best day of his life, and the smile on Krystal's face said it all—it told the story of Jesus transforming her heart forever. Krystal began sharing Scripture verses so that everyone could see the joy in her heart.

Krystal made an astounding impact in her twenty-one years on this earth. Although she was bound to a wheelchair, it did not hold her back from influencing many lives. From her school classmates to Pekka Rinne—then-goalie for the NHL's Nashville Predators—everyone who knew Krystal loved her. Krystal was active with the Nashville Predators Foundation and with Special Spaces—an organization that provides dream bedroom makeovers for children with cancer. She was an honorary part of the Vanderbilt University women's soccer team and countless other organizations. Krystal loved church, loved to worship, and enjoyed being a part of the college and young adult group. She had the ability to light up a room when she entered. Her joy was contagious, and her smile showed a heart at peace with Christ, as well as with herself.

At the funeral, James talked about how Krystal had received a bead for each cancer treatment she went through, whether that was chemo, radiation, or surgery. Each bead was a symbol of accomplishment for Krystal, as well as a marker of how far she had come. After seven years of brain cancer treatments, Krystal had accumulated quite a lot of beads. In fact, James held up her beads at the funeral, and they were strung together in a necklace that went from his head to the floor—twice. Krystal endured so much, but you would have never known it from her attitude. She was filled with joy and focused on what really mattered in life.

When the Make-A-Wish Foundation visited and asked Krystal what she wanted, she responded, "I'm good. Give my wish to someone else who really needs it." Then she gave them a donation.

We can learn many lessons from Krystal's life and journey:

- **Stand for the Kingdom.** The last time I saw Krystal stand up was November 4, 2018. Our church was in the midst of our "For the Kingdom" capital campaign. I asked everyone who was willing to commit to living their lives for God's Kingdom—for however long they had on this earth—to please stand. All across the room, people stood up. I looked over, and there was Krystal—struggling with all her might—rising up out of her wheelchair with her mother and father on each side. She stood! Boldly, bravely, she stood! When Krystal was laid to rest in her casket, she had her "For the Kingdom" ring on her finger and her baptism Bible in her arms. Today Krystal is standing in the presence of her Savior. May we, too, stand for His Kingdom.

- **Never complain.** If anyone had a reason to complain, it was Krystal—but she chose not to. She chose to focus on others and on Christ. I consider how often I complain about things that are trivial, yet my complaints feel like an insult to someone like Krystal, who endured so much more than me. We have a choice to make each day regarding how we will respond to the circumstances of life. Let's choose to give God glory and stand as Krystal did.

- **Share Jesus with others.** Krystal was passionate about sharing Jesus. She posted Scripture on her social media. She invited people to church. She didn't worry about what others might think about her; she just wanted them to meet the One who had changed her life. We should all be this passionate about Jesus. He is the One we all need. Instead of being self-focused, let's be Jesus-focused. Inviting someone to come to church or to know Jesus personally could transform their life for eternity.

- **Life is short, so make the most of it.** Twenty-one years seems like a short time to live, but so does seventy, eighty, or ninety years in the grand scheme of eternity. James 4:14 says, "You do not know what tomorrow will bring. What is your life? For you are a mist that appears for a little time and then vanishes." Let's make the most of what time we have. Be kind. Be generous. Live for Jesus. The *duration* of our lives isn't as important as the *donation* we make. (And I'm not just talking about a financial donation.)

Krystal is more alive today than ever before. In heaven she is free of her wheelchair and free of pain. She is before the throne of Jesus and worshiping Him with people from every nation and tribe. She is dancing with healthy legs, fully focused on the One who loves her more than any of us ever could. Krystal would want all of us to know Jesus today and to pursue what truly matters in life.

I miss my friend. I miss her smile and her joy, but I know this is not the end. I know that Krystal wouldn't want to spend eternity without us. So I pray that you, too, will follow Jesus. Meet the One whom Krystal loved. Make Jesus the joy of your life regardless of your circumstances, or especially *because of* your circumstances. And when your time comes, I pray you will be ready—ready to see Jesus and to hear Him say, "Well done, good and faithful servant" (Matthew 25:21). Krystal is home now, and she is whole. Thank you, Krystal, for modeling how to live this life well, for showing the rest of us how to overcome mountainous obstacles while serving Jesus and His people unselfishly and generously.

When you focus on your problems, they only seem to get bigger. If you are to live the life you were created to live, you need to focus on God and praise Him *through* your problems. Remember: It's not about the number of years you have been given on this earth. It's about what you do with them. Will you live for yourself, or will you live for God? Some of the people who've had the greatest impact on the world were not here for a lot of years. Conversely, many people live for eighty, ninety, or a hundred years and never make much of a difference. Use whatever time you have to live for God and to invest in His plan for you.

YOUR BODY IS A TEMPLE OF GOD

God has given us our physical bodies, but these bodies are temporary. They will eventually wear out. Whether we have twenty-one years, like Krystal, or a hundred years on this earth, at some point we will trade them in for new, resurrected bodies. Our eternal bodies will never wear out. There will be no more death. No more mourning, crying, or pain (see Revelation 21:4). Praise God! No more aches and pains. No more cancer. No more surgeries and lengthy recoveries. No more allergies. In the meantime, however, God tells us to take care of our earthly bodies.

The challenge is to resist focusing on ourselves. We can become obsessed with how we look and end up measuring our self-worth by our appearance. A fixation on our bodies is rampant in our culture today. In America alone, untold millions are spent every year on cosmetics and plastic surgery. Americans also spend like crazy on weight loss products. Our appearance can easily become our obsession.

We live in a *me*-focused society. We have our *i*Phones. We take countless *selfies*. The fashion industry not only tells us what to wear, but it then charges us top dollar to actually own those clothes. We spend hours every year trying to choose the right outfits. Then there is the cosmetics industry. Models show us what we could look like, or what we should look like. We spend so much money and time chasing the proverbial "fountain of youth" because we want to look better, to look younger, to look cooler. We're more focused on the external than the internal—not to mention the eternal.

While there are certainly good reasons to care for and maintain our bodies, we shouldn't let society at large dictate how we feel about ourselves. We should maintain our health. We should exercise and eat well. We need to be good stewards of the bodies we've been given, yet spending hours on social media comparing our looks with others is not a wise use of our time. We need to find our value and worth in what God says about us and not what the world says.

A woman recently came up to me after a service at our church. "You probably don't remember this," she said, "but last January you were talking about being physically healthy in the new year. You talked about the importance of taking care of our bodies but not becoming obsessed with them. You said that if you have not been to the doctor, then you need to go each year for an annual checkup. That you owe it to yourself and to your family. Well, I had not been to the doctor in over sixteen years, but I felt like God was telling me to go. So I made an appointment, and I went. When I did, they discovered the early stages of breast cancer. But because it was so early, they were able to do treatments. So here I stand today, nine months later, and I am cancer free."

Praise God!

Fear can actually hold us back from being healthy. We don't want to go to the doctor's office because *What if they find something?* We don't want to start working out because *What if I give up?* We don't want to deal with a weight issue because *What if I don't lose any weight?* We can't let fear keep us from taking care of our bodies. Schedule that doctor appointment. Go after the weight issue. Begin walking or doing some exercise each day. Don't become obsessed with it or allow it to define you—just let it help you become your best. The healthier you are, the more energy you'll have for what God has called you to!

God is sovereign over our lives. We are in His hands. He knows how long we will be on this earth and when He will take us home. In the meantime, we want to be at our best. We want to take care of our bodies so that we can give our all. We want to make use of modern medicine (that God has provided for us), eat healthy foods (that He has provided for us), and take care of these bodies (that He has provided for us) so that we can give Him our best. We want to be in good physical shape so we can help care for those who are sick, so we can volunteer for mission trips, so we can play with our grandchildren and ultimately help teach them about Jesus. We take care of our bodies, not so we can post great pictures, but so we can experience our best lives.

"Do you not know that your body is a temple of the Holy Spirit within you, whom you have from God? You are not your own, for you were bought with a price. So glorify God in your body" (1 Corinthians 6:19-20). We take care of the bodies we have been given so that we can glorify God with our bodies.

Whether you have twenty-one or ninety-one years on this earth, it's what you do with those years that really matters. So make the most of your time by focusing on what God says about your body, not what others say.

WHAT'S ON YOUR MIND?

Most people understand that eating healthy is important, but we often don't translate that logic to our thought lives. We know that what goes into the body matters. We like organic everything. We realize that if we eat only junk food, then we will eventually pay the price in our bodies. This same principle is also true when considering what goes into our minds. What if we were as diligent about what we put into our minds as we are about our bodies?

Change your thoughts, and you will change your life. If you fixate on negative thoughts all day and just chew on those, then negative thoughts will likely come out in your life. If you focus on what popular culture says you should do, if you compare yourself with pictures on social media, or if you allow worry to take over your mind, then you will live with ongoing fear, regret, and stress. This is not the way you were meant to live.

The mental aspect of living beyond the ordinary is vital. Fill your mind with the things of God and with what He says about you. When you do this, you'll grow in confidence. You'll grow stronger, both mentally and physically. You'll be better prepared to take on the challenges of life—whether it is parenting a toddler or battling cancer. The Bible urges us to "take every thought captive to obey Christ"

(2 Corinthians 10:5). This is where the battle of the mind is fought and won. Begin to fill your mind with the things of God. Memorize key Bible passages. When the enemy tries to get a foothold in your mind, focus instead on what God has to say.

Hebrews 12:1-2 tells us, "Therefore, since we are surrounded by so great a cloud of witnesses, let us also lay aside every weight, and sin which clings so closely, and let us run with endurance the race that is set before us, looking to Jesus, the founder and perfecter of our faith, who for the joy that was set before him endured the cross, despising the shame, and is seated at the right hand of the throne of God."

In the race of life we are surrounded by people who have gone before us. Included in that great cloud of witnesses are people like Peter, John, and the other disciples along with godly people from all generations. That group includes people you know and love—maybe your grandmother or great-grandmother. Maybe your mom or dad. Maybe a best friend or a godly mentor.

In my case, my dad is already in heaven. My father grew up on a farm and played baseball. He went into the air force and then on to college. Church and faith were not a priority for him until he met my mother. My mom led my dad to the Lord, and my dad became very passionate about Jesus. My dad worked in business, but his true joy was investing in God's Kingdom and in church. We bonded over sports, but through all my time in youth sports, my father made sure we were in church and growing in the Lord. My dad went home to be with Jesus about five years ago, and I still miss him. But I know I will see him again.

Once again, Hebrews 12:1 tells us to "lay aside every weight, and sin which clings so closely." In other words, we must lay aside everything that will slow us down in becoming all God intends for us to be. If there is sin in your life, confess it. Don't think you will accomplish all that God desires if you persist in doing things that He specifically says not to do. God is not trying to keep you from enjoying life—just the opposite: God wants you to have the most abundant life. God also wants you to live without regrets. He wants you to reach your full potential. He doesn't want you weighed down by the consequences of bad decisions.

How do you do this? Fix your eyes on Jesus! That's it. Where your focus is, there your life will go. Focus on the One who created you and the One who sustains you. Examine what you allow into your mind and heart. Consider the media that you consume. Pay attention to what you take in through your eyes and your ears, since it all ends up in your mind. Everything matters.

WHERE'S YOUR FOCUS?

We have all likely heard Proverbs 23:7: "For as he thinks in his heart, so is he" (NKJV). This is so true. What dominates your thoughts? If it is making money, then that will control your life. It will be your desire and passion. You will make other decisions based on your focus, but at what cost to your life?

If your focus is pleasure, then you will live for pleasure. You will see other people as objects to please you. Your life will be dominated by a desire to please yourself. But if your focus is God, then you will make decisions based on who He wants you to become. You will live for His agenda and not your own.

If we are honest with ourselves, many times our focus is not God but rather what others think about us. When we focus on what others think, we end up living with envy, worry, and fear. When we focus on what God says about us, we see that God says we are enough. We are redeemed. We are loved. We are His sons and daughters.

Jesus said it this way: "Seek first his kingdom and his righteousness, and all these things will be given to you as well" (Matthew 6:33, NIV). Focusing on the eternal should be the goal of your life. Keep in mind that the goal is not simply going to heaven—that will come automatically if you are a Christ-follower and have received God's grace and forgiveness through Jesus. Heaven is the *reward*, not the goal. The goal is God. He is the object of our pursuit. He is our one desire. If we can focus each day on Him and live for His agenda, we will begin to move past the ordinary. That does not mean that everything will be perfect, of course. We will still experience hard times and struggles. In fact, it's through those difficulties that God grows and refines us. And it is in those struggles that we grow deeper and stronger in God.

I love how Jesus says to focus on God, "and all these things will be given to you as well." What are "all these things"? Some of them are the things that we so often take for granted—what we will eat, what we will drink, what we will wear. But Jesus tells us not to worry about such things. As Christ-followers, we are instructed to seek God and His righteousness first. It's a vital part of living an extraordinary life.

BLESS OTHERS

To fulfill our purpose, we need to work on being our personal best as well as being a blessing to others. We need to understand that we are not competing against others like we do in sports, but we are called instead to make those around us better. We grow when others grow. We are blessed when others are blessed. It is a countercultural concept these days, but it remains the truth. Ordinary people try to outperform others, while those living extraordinary lives are blessing and assisting others.

As you consider what God wants to do in you and through you, look for ways you can use what has been given to you to help others. You have been blessed not just for your own benefit, but so that you will be a blessing to those around you. Keep in mind that we never "fully arrive." There is always a new dream to dream and a new way to bless and help others.

At the end of your life, you can't take anything with you. You might have seen the bumper sticker that reads, "He who dies with the most toys still dies." You can't hold on to any of the money, possessions, or stuff you have amassed. But what you can do is love God and love others. You can keep pursuing your goals and blessing others all along the way. You can leave the world a richer and fuller place because you made a difference. And you will have all eternity to celebrate God's goodness in your life and in the lives of others.

Consider that there are more than six hundred laws mentioned in the Old Testament. That's a lot. Can you imagine the effort necessary to simply remember all those laws, much less try to keep all of them? But then Jesus came along, and one day a man asked Him, "Teacher, which is the great commandment in the Law?" (Matthew 22:36). Jesus' reply was incredible! Out of more than six hundred laws, Jesus boiled down for everyone what is the greatest, most important commandment of all: "You shall love the Lord your God with all your heart and with all your soul and with all your mind" (Matthew 22:37).

Jesus told us to get things right with God. To put Him first. Not just to obey some of His commands, but to love Him with all our heart, soul, and mind. As Jesus said, God's commands are really all about love—loving God and loving others.

But Jesus kept going. Remember, the man asked for *one* law—"the great commandment"—but Jesus continued: "This is the great and first commandment. And a second is like it: You shall love your neighbor as yourself" (Matthew 22:38-39). Jesus told us that our vertical relationship with God is most important, then went on to say that our horizontal relationships with others are also critical. How we love God is demonstrated in how we love others.

People who live their best lives love God—they are growing in their relationship with their Creator—and they love others. If you have a best friend, you naturally want to spend time together. This is how your relationship grows. It's the same way with God. Spend time with Him. Put your faith and trust in Him. Recognize that God knows what is best for you, both now and in the future. None of us knows the future, but we can know Who holds the future.

People who move past the ordinary don't spend their time comparing themselves with others, complaining about others, or holding grudges. These people forgive and offer grace, just as they, too, have received forgiveness and grace.

"Love your neighbor as yourself" is central to Jesus' teaching. That's because most people know about God and know that they should love others, but they struggle with the part about loving themselves. "Love your neighbor as yourself" means that you should also love yourself. Do you love yourself? If not, you are not alone. Many people focus on all the things they've decided are wrong with themselves—their nose is too big, their ears are too small, they don't have enough money, they've made too many mistakes, they don't have the thing they think they need. People who live extraordinary lives, however, have learned to love themselves.

I'm not talking about a self-centered, narcissistic love, but a genuine appreciation for the person God created. If you can develop a real appreciation for who God created you to be, then it will impact every other facet of your life. Maybe your struggles in your close relationships—with your spouse, your boss, your kids, your friends, your parents—are not really about those other people. Maybe those struggles stem from you not feeling good about yourself. Think about it.

AN ART TEACHER

My wife, Lisa, grew up in a small town, and many of the people born there never leave. Lisa was a skilled basketball player in school, but God also gave her a love and a gift for art. She thrived on the court and in the art room. Her senior year of high school, she decided to skip basketball so she could concentrate on her art. "What will you ever do with art?" her basketball coach asked. "What will I ever do with basketball?" Lisa responded. Now, some people can earn a scholarship for basketball or even make it a career, but Lisa knew that was not for her. God put another passion in her heart.

No one in Lisa's family had ever gone to college. Lisa's dad was not in favor of her attending college. He wanted Lisa to stay in their small town. But Lisa was blessed with an art teacher at her small high school who believed in her. This teacher loved God and loved her students. Unbeknownst to

Lisa, her art teacher sent examples of Lisa's art to some major universities. The teacher worked tirelessly after hours to help Lisa earn a scholarship to a particular university. Lisa's dad never thought it would happen, but it did.

Lisa excelled at that university. After graduating, she moved to Nashville and began a successful career as a graphic designer and art director. Lisa's career opened doors for photo shoots in England, Japan, Israel, and other countries around the world. She has designed magazines, brochures, logos, and newsletters for major corporations and nonprofits. Lisa has an incredible career in art because God blessed her with a gift she pursued with a passion, and because an art teacher believed in her.

What a difference this teacher made in the life of my wife, our children, our church, and more! That art teacher was a Christ-follower, and she was living out her faith—not only in her classroom, but in each day of her life. Her obedience to God impacted her life and the lives of many others.

When you live your extraordinary life, you encourage those around you to live extraordinary lives as well. The word *encourage* basically means "inspire with courage." When you follow the example of Lisa's art teacher, you inspire your children, your students, your coworkers, your neighbors, and others with courage. We have been given a challenge: "Encourage one another and build one another up" (1 Thessalonians 5:11). Let's be encouragers. We can all make a difference. In fact, you might never know how many people you impact in your life.

Someday, in eternity, I believe people will thank you for living your extraordinary life—people you never had a clue about. Your obedience to God affects more than just you.

We all need someone to believe in us. God believes in you, and I do as well. You can live the life you were created to live. In the process, you'll have opportunities to believe in someone else. Be that art teacher who changes a young person's life. Believe in your kids, your grandkids, and all those whom God puts in your path. Encourage those you meet to live the life they were created to live. Pray for them. Write to them. Give them a copy of this book! Go out of your way to make someone else's life better. You can impact the world one life at a time. Everyone needs someone to believe in them.

Renowned evangelist Billy Graham once said, "We are not cisterns made for hoarding; we are channels made for sharing." We have been blessed as Christ-followers, and we can and should share our blessings with others. Consider whom you can bless. Think about your spouse, children, roommates, relatives, coworkers, or neighbors—or perhaps even children in another country. I challenge and encourage you to make a difference. As you bless others, you are blessed in return. Someone once invested in you, and now you have a chance to encourage someone else to reach their full potential.

OPENHANDED PRAYER

A habit that helps me focus on God is to pray with open hands. If you want to try this, simply open your hands and place them in front of you. Then begin to pray: *God, I want more of You. Fill me with Your love, grace, and knowledge. I openhandedly give my life to You.* Then turn your open hands over and pray: *God, empty me of sin, resentment, bitterness— anything in my life that is not of You. Empty me of the fears, worries, and anxieties that keep me from reaching my full potential in You.* Finally, turn your open hands back over and pray: *God, I give You my life. I want to live the life You have for me. Fill me with Your Spirit. I am Yours.* This is a great way to focus on God and commit your day—and your life—to Him.

5
INVEST
WISELY

Life's most persistent and urgent question
is, "What are you doing for others?"

MARTIN LUTHER KING JR.

MANY TIMES LIFE FEELS LIKE A MOVIE, one in which we are the star of the show. Everything revolves around us. But the truth is that we are just a small part of God's incredible story. It's our privilege to invest in others and see lives changed. Let me share with you an example of how I've seen this happen.

Tudor grew up as an orphan in Balti, Moldova. When our first mission team from Rolling Hills went to serve in that orphanage about thirteen years ago, we met twelve-year-old Tudor. At first he was quiet and distant. He wouldn't engage. As the week progressed, he became more rebellious. While the other orphaned children participated in group activities, Tudor stood apart. When people tried to get close to him, he walked or ran away. Tudor had obviously suffered trauma, so he pushed others away.

During the next year's visit it was clear that Tudor longed for attention, but he didn't know how to get it. He wanted to participate, but as one of the older kids, he also wanted to look cool in front of the others.

As children in these state-run orphanages move closer to age fifteen or sixteen, at which point they are forced to leave, they often begin acting out. They face the fear of not knowing what will happen to them since, as true orphans, they literally have no other place to go. Many of the orphaned boys end up in organized crime, prison, or worse. And many of the girls end up being trafficked. These kids are so vulnerable. Tudor, feeling this pressure, acted out—to the point that he tried to set one of our team member's pants on fire!

The next year, we launched JMI—Justice & Mercy International—through Rolling Hills as a way to help these vulnerable children. Through our sponsorship program, we paired a solid believer from our church or somewhere else in the United States with a child in Moldova. Then we hired Moldovan translators to help keep up with the sponsored children and translate letters from their sponsors. The goal was to bring godly mentors into the kids' lives since they didn't have any parents to go to for advice, comfort, support, or encouragement. The sponsors also supported the children financially to help provide food, clothing, and educational opportunities.

An incredible woman from our church named Becky

became Tudor's sponsor. This was a gift from God to Tudor—and to Becky. The next year, through JMI, we launched our first transitional living home. The Grace House is located in Chisinau, the capital city of Moldova, and it houses girls who come from the orphanages. This transitional living program gives them a place to live after they age out of the orphanages, and it is a life-changing opportunity for each and every one of them.

While there are other wonderful ministries like IJM (International Justice Mission) that work to free trafficked girls from brothels all over the world, we at JMI decided to operate on the prevention side of the equation. We knew that if we could provide a safe place for children to live during the time when they are most susceptible, then we, by God's grace, could help prevent them from going through this horror. And we could see it working, as these young women were coming to know Christ and becoming confident leaders.

After two years of operating the Grace House for girls, we realized that we also needed a place for boys. We launched the Boys 2 Leaders program in another house in Chisinau. With so many children needing a safe home, our team in Moldova had to institute an application process for girls and boys who wanted to participate.

Becky shared with Tudor about the program and encouraged him to apply. His time at the orphanage was coming to an end, and he had nowhere else to go. Tudor did apply, but because of his attitude at the orphanage and his lack of initiative in his studies, he was not accepted. Our staff encouraged him to apply for a job (although the average salary in Moldova is only around $300 a month) or to enroll at a trade school that would provide housing.

On the day the van came to pick up the boys and girls who had been accepted to the transitional living program, Tudor also showed up. The van driver was simply hired to drive, so he did not know who had been selected. Tudor, carrying all his possessions in a small plastic bag, got into the vehicle with everyone else. After a two-hour van ride, they arrived in Chisinau. Alina, our national director in Moldova, was there to greet everyone, and she was surprised to see Tudor! She knew he had not been selected, but her heart went out to him. By God's grace, an extra bed had recently been added to the house, so Alina told Tudor he could stay.

Tudor changed dramatically in the Boys 2 Leaders program. He committed his life to Christ and—with the help of Becky and Igor, the Boys 2 Leaders director—was able to get into college. There Tudor excelled academically, and his entire attitude changed. After his first year, he began to learn English. He wanted to spend time with every mission team possible in order to return to the orphanages and help other children. After two years, he became a leader in the Boys 2 Leaders program, and then he was asked to stay a third year as an associate leader under Igor!

On our latest trip to Moldova, many of us were there to celebrate as Tudor stood at the altar and married Stella, a young woman who had stayed at the Grace House. Becky was there, as well as countless others who had watched God transform Tudor's life. Tudor and Stella both graduated from the transitional living program and now work for JMI in Moldova. God is using them to speak at orphanages all over the country to tell other precious children about the love of God and the help they can receive through Jesus and JMI. Our God is using them in unbelievable ways, and I am so proud of them!

People want to see God do wonders, don't they? They want a sign that God is real. They say, "If Jesus only did miracles today like He did in the Bible, then we would believe in Him." Yet I believe that God is doing wonders every day. We can see them in the changed lives all around us. As God changes hearts, we see God at work.

As we share God's truth with our children or children around the world, we get to see how His love changes lives. The story goes on—Tudor, Stella, Becky, and all of us at Rolling Hills are praying for and sharing God's love with others. I'm so thankful for what our God is doing at our church and through Justice & Mercy International. Let's keep praying, investing, going, and serving for His glory. And may God pour out His blessings on Tudor and Stella in their marriage. Their amazing story together is just beginning, and I can't wait to see what God will continue to do through them!

SEEING GOD WORK

I want to tell you what I think is a miraculous story about one of our visits to Moldova. It was our last night in the country, and after an amazing week of running two camps for orphaned and vulnerable children in the village of Carpineni, we gathered at the Grace House in Chisinau for a dinner with the girls living there. The Grace House was our first purchase in Moldova through Justice & Mercy International. The large, three-story building is home to fourteen girls who were forced to leave their orphanage at the age of fifteen or sixteen. These girls have three years to live there, continuing to attend school while they grow in Christ. It is a place where lives change, and you can sense God's presence there.

The night of our gathering, a young man named Sava came up to share his story in front of a living room filled with close to one hundred people—twenty-five Americans from our church at Rolling Hills, about forty-five young people from our transitional programs (the Grace House and Boys 2 Leaders homes) and from our independent living and graduate programs (people living in JMI apartments and attending college or university), plus our JMI Moldova team of about twenty wonderful servants of Christ.

Nineteen-year-old Sava had been part of our Boys 2 Leaders home for three years. He walked to the front of the room, sat down in a chair, and faced the rest of us. His back was to the front door, and we all sat on the floor waiting to hear his story. He rubbed his hands together nervously, trying to determine how to begin. When he finally spoke, Sava said his first memory was when his mother dropped him off at the orphanage at just three years old. He was scared and alone. Sava's mom said she would come back to see him, but she never did. Other kids had family members show up every now and then, but no one ever showed up for him.

Sava said he remembered being a bad kid. He refused to study or do any schoolwork. Whenever a teacher called on him, Sava never knew the right answer. Some of the teachers at the orphanage would hit him. Some hit him repeatedly. On one occasion Sava recalled standing in front of the class. The teacher asked him a question, and when he didn't know the answer, the teacher slammed Sava's head into the blackboard!

When Sava was about ten years old, a social worker informed him that he had a brother. He never knew he had a brother. The woman said Sava's brother was in an orphanage in the north and would like to come see him. Sava was excited to hear this. He waited eagerly, but months went by and his brother didn't show up.

About a year later, Sava was sitting in class and looking out the window when he saw the same social worker drive up. He noticed a young man in the car with her, and he wondered if this was his brother at last. Sure enough, it *was* his brother!

And his name was Tudor.

As they talked that day, Tudor told him that they had two other brothers, and he said that maybe they could all meet one day. Before Tudor departed, he told Sava that he believed in him and that he should do his best.

"That was the day," Sava shared, "that I started to study and try harder in school."

Another year passed, and the same social worker called the orphanage to speak with Sava. The social worker asked him over the phone, "Sava, if you could say anything to your mother, what would it be?"

"I was so excited," Sava told us. "I thought I was finally going to see my mom again." He told the social worker that he didn't know what he would say. She asked him again: "Sava, if you could say anything to your mother, what would it be?" He thought for a moment and finally said, "Mom, I'm sorry. I have missed you. I want to see you." Yet the social worker said, "Well, Sava, your mother died, and I am coming tomorrow to pick you up so you can go to the funeral and say your last words to her."

"I just stood there and cried," Sava said.

Just as she had said, the social worker showed up the next day with Tudor in the car. Together they went to the funeral. While they were there, Tudor told Sava about a program he was in called Boys 2 Leaders through Justice & Mercy International. Tudor told Sava about living in a house in Chisinau with a lot of other guys and about meeting Jesus. He told him what a difference the program had made in his life and that maybe Sava could be a part of it one day. First, however, he would have to do well in school.

"The more he talked," Sava recounted, "the more I wanted to be a part of it." He returned to the orphanage and soon became one of the best students. Sava worked hard and tried to be friends with everyone. His teachers could scarcely believe the turnaround in Sava's life. When it came time to graduate, he applied for the Boys 2 Leaders program and was accepted. He cried again, he said, but this time it was because he was so excited.

By the time Sava moved into the Boys 2 Leaders house, Tudor had moved on to an independent living situation. But Tudor came by the house often, looking out for Sava. Tudor also introduced Sava to Becky, his American sponsor through JMI. Becky continued to communicate with Tudor and helped him with clothes, food, and decisions in life. Becky was like a mother to Tudor.

When he finally met Becky, Sava said, "I asked her if she would be my mom as well. And she said yes!" Through tears, Sava told the roomful of people: "I don't know where I would be in life, or if I would even be alive, without JMI. God has come into my heart and has given me people like Becky, Igor, and others from Rolling Hills to help me." He added, "I want to thank God, and I want to thank my brother for saving me."

As only God can orchestrate, at this moment Tudor (who had been helping translate at another location) walked through the front door and stood behind Sava. By this time we were all in tears. We were hearing about—and seeing—God at work. We were witnesses to salvation and redemption.

Sava served alongside us as we ran the camps in Carpineni. He helped lead worship and translated for our Bible studies as we shared the Good News of Christ with precious orphaned children just like him. He prayed for transforming change in the lives of hundreds of children, just as his life had been transformed. God gave us a front row seat to the birth of a future spiritual leader.

I will forever be grateful for that night in the Grace House. For the chance to see God's hand on this young man and his brother standing behind him, with all of us surrounding him. It will remain forever etched in my mind. I am confident that Sava will do great things for the Kingdom. I thank God that I've been able to watch His church at Rolling Hills praying for, giving to, and visiting this country of Moldova for fifteen years and counting. I am thankful that Justice & Mercy International has been able to share God's love with orphaned kids like Sava.

These seeds of the gospel, first planted in young hearts through the years, are now flourishing in strong spiritual leaders. This is how God changes an orphan, a nation, and a lot of Americans along the way. Praise God for the hope we have in Christ and for the lives that He has transformed for His glory! Thank You, God, for Sava and for the many like him who now have "a future and a hope" (see Jeremiah 29:11).

This is what it means to invest in others. Mission teams from the United States invested by visiting orphanages in Moldova. One of the people on those teams, a woman named Becky, invested in a young man named Tudor. Tudor invested in his younger brother Sava, and Sava now goes back to the orphanages and invests in other orphaned children. This is the impact that results from investment. When you invest in someone, it makes a ripple in the pond. Those ripples continue to spread out and impact others—others you might never meet this side of heaven. What a difference we can make when we invest in others!

THE GOLDEN RULE

When Jesus gave us the Golden Rule (see Matthew 7:12 and Luke 6:31), it was radical. Almost everyone today knows this principle, which in its most popular phrasing says, "Do unto others as you would have them do unto you." Even those who don't know its scriptural basis still know the gist of the rule and have probably quoted it to others (most likely to their children).

In ancient literature, however, a different version of this saying was in use before Jesus ever walked the earth. The older version was in the negative form: "Don't do to others as you would not like them to do to you." If you think about it, this makes sense too. If you don't want someone to steal your things, then don't steal theirs. If you don't want someone to hurt a loved one of yours, then don't hurt one of theirs.

But Jesus turned this ancient saying into a positive: "*Do* unto others . . ." In other words, be proactive. Take the initiative. If you see a need, meet it. If you see someone in trouble, step in and help. After all, if you were in trouble, you would want someone to help you. Jesus' version changes everything. No longer should we live in fear and isolation. We are called to actively help others. In other words, don't sit on the sidelines—get in the game! Many people live passive lives, yet Jesus invites us to get involved and make a difference in the lives of others. When people see this sort of behavior, they see Christ in us.

What difference can you make in someone else's life? Start at home. God placed you in the family you are in for a reason. God gave you the roommate or the suitemates you have for a reason. Share God's love where you're at. If there's a need at home and you can meet it, then do so. The people around you are not just there to serve you or to simply exist. You are there to impact *them*. Love them well. So begin in your home, then look to branch out. Ask God every day, "What can I do for others?"

View your coworkers as people to love and serve rather than as inconveniences. Ask others how you can pray for them. Demonstrate God's love in simple ways. Look around your neighborhood. If you find out someone is sick, take him or her a meal. Don't expect anything in return, just do it. Be a light.

After meeting the needs in your neighborhood, try visiting a place less fortunate. Learn the needs in your larger community. Then consider going international. Whether it's Moldova, the Amazon jungle, or some other far-flung location on the map—go! Go to share God's love and to serve. An amazing thing that often happens when you help others is that *you* are the one who is changed the most. When you invest in others, God changes you. He changes you to be more like Jesus.

Mother Teresa was famously quoted as saying, "Spread love wherever you go. Let no one ever come to you without leaving happier." We would all do well to adopt the same attitude. Look for ways to invest in others. Your spouse or your roommates or your friends—how can you encourage them today? Your children, grandchildren, nieces, or nephews—how can you show them love today? Your coworkers—how can you make their jobs easier?

You might be surprised how your life will change when you take the focus off yourself. Your attitude and others' opinions of you will change as well. People need help and hope, and God intentionally put you in the place where you live and with the people you have around you. So invest in others, and watch God work.

We can all help make a difference, whether big or small. As I shared in the opening chapter, Dolly Parton was aware of illiteracy in the community where she grew up and decided to do something about it. She started the Imagination Library, which gives a book to every family when they have a baby. Not just one book, but a book every month for the first five years of the child's life. Every child born in the state of Tennessee is eligible for the Imagination Library, and the program is expanding nationally and internationally! I am so thankful for Dolly's generous investment in others.

Maybe God has given you a vision to invest in others through teaching. Maybe it's through being a parent. Maybe it's through your workplace or community. Maybe it's through service to others. Your impact can be life-changing for someone. If you're a parent, for example, consider the ripple effect on the rest of the family: You can invest in your kids, who can invest in their kids, who can invest in their kids.

After just a few generations, you have the potential to impact children and grandchildren and great-grandchildren, who in turn can impact thousands of people. Yet the size of your calling isn't as important as recognizing the vision God has given you and having the faithfulness to live it out. God just wants willing hearts—hearts through which He can develop the extraordinary that's already inside you.

BECOME DISCIPLINED WITH TIME AND MONEY

Sometimes we want to invest in others, but we don't have the time or resources. This is where we must become more disciplined with both. If you want to know what you value, then pay attention to how and where you spend your time and your money. If you spend these two limited resources only on yourself and your own desires, then you need to reconsider your priorities.

The hard truth is that a lot of us spend time comparing ourselves with others—our houses, cars, kids, degrees, financial statuses, looks, and a whole lot more. People in marketing are geniuses about this. You didn't even know you needed that new product until you saw the commercial. Then you noticed that a neighbor had one, at which point you became obsessed with it. How many things do we buy that we hardly ever use simply because we thought they would elevate us in the eyes of others?

This is what ordinary people do. They spend their time consumed with what other people think of them. (At the same time, most of those same people are not thinking of others, but of themselves.) Part of finding the *extra* in extraordinary living is recognizing that everything we have comes from God. We are simply stewards of what He has given us. God has promised to meet our needs and to take care of us. The reason He sometimes gives us more is so that we can help take care of others.

I know it's a cliché, but if we don't learn to control our time and money, then our time and money will control us. This means we must prioritize. There are plenty of "time bandits" ready and willing to rob us of our time, yet taking back control in this area is so liberating. Freedom comes when you prioritize time with God, family, and close friends, plus a bit of margin in your schedule so that God can use you.

You don't need to buy into the cultural norm of living an overcrowded and overscheduled existence. When someone asks us how we are doing, we often respond, "Well, I am *incredibly* busy." As if being worn out is a badge of honor! We need to be busy doing the right things, not just busy for the sake of it. There is a difference between activity and accomplishment. As you look at your current schedule, are you accomplishing the things in life that you want to accomplish? Are you investing the time you do have in ways that help others and further the things that really matter?

We often say, "If I only had more time, I would . . ." *I would serve others. I would spend time with my children. I would volunteer to help make my community better. I would get to know my neighbors.* But would you? Would you really? The fact is that we all have the same amount of time each day, each week, each year. So how is it that some people accomplish so much while others accomplish so little? You need to take control of your time. It's up to you to set priorities and invest the time you have been given. It's vital that you first make note of how you currently spend your time. Are there any changes you need to make? If so, make them.

The same issues exist with money. Once again, it's a question of who's in control. We all have bills and expenses. Lots of us get to the end of the month only to wonder where all the money went. We never seem to have "enough." And we likely never will. In all my years of working with and counseling people, I have never heard someone say, "I have enough money." Instead they say, "I need more money!" The late rapper The Notorious B.I.G. had it right: "Mo Money" leads to "Mo Problems."

Isn't it the truth? We figure if we could just win the lottery, then all our problems would be solved. But look at people who have won the lottery—they often have more problems! Long-lost friends and relatives come out of the woodwork wanting a share of the prize. And of course the winners want to buy a few things. Who wouldn't? But they often end up buying too many cars or a house that's too big, only to discover that they don't have enough money to take care of their new possessions. And that doesn't even take into account all the taxes on their winnings! Instead of counting on the lottery, we're better off learning how to manage the money we do have and investing it wisely.

Once more, it's a matter of priorities. If we believe that God promises to meet all our basic needs, then we must also believe that what He has entrusted to us at this moment is enough. If we need more, then He will provide it at the right time. Most of us look at money as a scarcity product—once it's gone, it's gone for good. But God looks at it as a constant flow. When we invest it in things that matter, then there is growth—both in others and in us. Here's my favorite principle when it comes to money: "10, 10, 80." Your first 10 percent you give. That is a biblical principle called *tithing*. When you attend church, either in person or online, then your first 10 percent goes to God's church to be invested in helping others.

The second 10 percent you save. This allows you to build up savings for a house, a car, emergencies, medical expenses, retirement, and so on.

You then live on the remaining 80 percent. Restricting your spending this way helps you live below your means—which is another countercultural concept, but a very wise one. Ordinary people live on about 120 percent of what they make. How does that work? Well, it doesn't. Ordinary people spending more than they make helps explain why so many folks today are in debt. I sound like a broken record here, but if we don't learn to control money, then money will control us.

Learning to handle our money wisely changes everything, but it isn't easy. Money can be difficult to manage when it feels like we never have enough. The key, I've discovered, is not necessarily how much money you have (or don't have), but what you do with that money. We can't effectively learn how to budget our resources unless we know where our money is going.

If you feel overwhelmed by debt, don't wait around and simply hope that things will get better. Make a plan to address this issue right away, and that includes making a budget you can actually live with! Even more importantly, ask God to help you stick to it. When you learn how to live without debt, you are no longer allowing money to control you; you are telling your money where to go. Talk about liberating!

When you finally have control over your money—and, to a certain extent, your time—it's much easier to find the mental, relational, and financial margin to invest in others. You are no longer living for money, but for loving your neighbor. That's what God wants you to do; you just need to do it. Remember that everything you have on this earth stays here. So let's invest in the eternal.

Pour into others and watch God change lives. You might discover along the way that your own life is the one that changes the most. The people I know who are living beyond the ordinary are all generous, and not just 10 percent generous. These people have created margins with time and money so that when they see a need, they can meet it. They invest in others and not just in themselves. Helping others brings you a sense of joy. When you see people's lives impacted for the better, it fills you up with joy in return.

The most quoted verse in the Bible says, "For God so loved the world, that he gave . . ." (John 3:16). God *gave*. He gave what was most precious to Him, His Son, so that you and I could have eternal life. God invested in us, and He invites us to do the same for others.

THE STORY OF A MODERN RICH YOUNG RULER

I will never forget when a young husband asked if he could meet with me. I'll call him Kenneth. By all outward appearances, everything was going great in Kenneth's life. He had a successful business and a beautiful wife, and they had recently dedicated their first child at church. So when we met, I was truly surprised by what I heard.

Kenneth told me that he was more than $300,000 in debt due to sports gambling. *How could this happen?* I wondered.

"Does your wife know?" I asked. Kenneth was stoic as he talked about how his wife had found out after he had covered it up as long as he could. He had borrowed money from family, friends, and others to feed his gambling habit. We talked, we prayed, and we set him up for counseling in order to get help. It was heartbreaking to see the hurt and pain Kenneth's sin had caused in his family, but he had confessed and seemed to be on the path to healing.

About a year later, however, Kenneth made another appointment with me. This time he informed me that he'd gotten caught again. "What?" I said. "I thought you were doing better and moving forward." But no—he had only tried to cover up the sin. Kenneth had continued gambling and was now even deeper in debt. His wife, who was six months pregnant with their second child, had discovered what was happening. He was once more asking for my advice.

"Let me ask you something," I said. "Are you sorry that you got caught, or are you really repenting this time?" Kenneth was a bit taken aback. But I (or the Holy Spirit working through me) kept pressing. "You see, until you are really ready to repent and get right with the Lord, you will keep doing this. You will keep gambling, and you will keep hurting yourself and your family, until you get caught again. You need to genuinely repent before the Lord. You need to be truly broken over your sin and commit your life fully to Him."

I questioned Kenneth further: "Why do you think you keep doing this?"

"I want to have what everyone else has," he responded. "I want to be rich. I want to have nice cars. I want people to look up to me and think I am important."

"Have you ever heard of the rich young ruler?" I asked.

Matthew 19, Mark 10, and Luke 18 each recount the story of a guy who ran up to Jesus. He was rich (like

Kenneth wanted to be), young (also like Kenneth), and a ruler (Kenneth was a successful company owner). This guy came up to Jesus because it was clear that, despite everything he had going for him, his life was still not fulfilling. So the young man said to Jesus, "What must I do to inherit eternal life?" (Mark 10:17). Notice the "I do." This is how most of us instinctively think: We assume eternal life is about what *we* do, when it is actually about what *He* has done. Jesus paid the price for us to have eternal life.

Their conversation didn't last long, probably because Jesus already knew what had a hold of this guy's heart. He told him, "Go, sell all that you have and give to the poor" (Mark 10:21). (Notice that this is the only place in Scripture where Jesus says this, so this message is likely not a universal message for all—yet we *are* all called to be generous and to avoid the love of money.) I love how, right before Christ answered the man's question, it says, "Jesus, looking at him, loved him" (Mark 10:21). Jesus loved this young ruler, yet the man walked away from Jesus. And Scripture says that "he went away sorrowful, for he had great possessions" (Mark 10:22). Money, it turned out, was this man's god.

I've always wondered what happened to this man. Did he ever regret walking away? I'm guessing he did. We know the names of people who left everything to follow Jesus—people like Matthew, who was a wealthy tax collector. Guys like Peter, Andrew, James, and John, who ran a fishing business. But when Jesus invited James and John to follow Him, the Bible says, "Immediately they left the boat and their father and followed him" (Matthew 4:22). Jesus provided for them, and they saw God do miracles in their generation.

All we know about the guy who walked away is that he was a rich young ruler. He lived his allotted number of years, and then, unless he had a change of heart, he spent eternity apart from God. That's so sad. He missed it! He could have been generous, impacting other people, witnessing lives changed dramatically, experiencing the joy of being in fellowship with other believers, even watching Jesus do miracles and being filled with awe and wonder. But instead he missed out. He settled for what the world had to offer, and he walked away filled with sorrow.

As for Kenneth, I asked him to make a similar choice—did he want to be a "rich young ruler" or a disciple of Jesus? Would he live for himself or live for Jesus, his family, and others? Kenneth sat there for a moment in silence, feeling the weight of the question. He said he had to think about it, and then he left.

Jesus doesn't call everyone who wants to follow Him to "go, sell all that you have and give to the poor," but if He did, could you? Keep in mind that everything we have already belongs to Him!

Our faith is not in money but in God, who richly provides everything we need. We are called to live for God and not for worldly success. God more than takes care of us, and we use the resources He has entrusted to us to further His Kingdom. To love people. To care for ourselves and others. To make an eternal difference. This is how our lives move from ordinary to extraordinary. This is how we experience joy, peace, and purpose.

I'm pleased to tell you that about two weeks later, Kenneth came back to see me. This time he bounded into my office. With a huge smile on his face, he gave me the biggest hug ever. "I did it!" he exclaimed. "I fully committed my life to Jesus!"

Kenneth went on to tell me that he talked to his wife and apologized to her, they prayed together with the entire family, and then he got on his knees and asked Jesus to be his Lord and Savior. He said he knew it would be hard, but he was willing to do whatever needed to be done to pay back his debts, provide for his family, and live the rest of his life for Jesus. Every day matters. Every decision matters. Kenneth's best life was just beginning.

6
CHOOSE JOY

We cannot cure the world of sorrows,
but we can choose to live in joy.
JOSEPH CAMPBELL

"I'M SO SORRY," I SAID. "I can't understand you."

It was Christmas Eve. I was in the midst of a large group of people, and a woman in her early sixties was gripping my hands. We were surrounded by her extended family—her husband, children, grandchildren, cousins, and so on—and I kept trying to grasp what she was saying. Her Parkinson's had taken a toll to the point where it was difficult to understand her.

The woman was clearly struggling to speak. It seemed to me like she was feeling the hurt of her disease and the life she was missing. I held her hands and repeated what I thought she had said: "Yes, I'm so sorry too. You have an amazing family." Her husband looked at me and said, "No, what she is saying is 'I am so blessed.'" Seeing her faith in Jesus, and her family standing beside her, loving her, I knew. *She is right. She is blessed.*

Joy is a choice. Joy was her choice. Every day that we wake up, we can choose joy. Our attitude impacts everything. If we believe it's going to be a great day, then there's a great chance that it will be. In much the same way, if we believe it's going to be a terrible day, then it probably will be.

That's why we should choose joy every day. The Bible is filled with verses relating to joy. It's a fruit of the Spirit, it's contagious, and it can be very healing! Understanding that God made you and created you for a reason can fill you with joy and change your attitude for the better.

There is a difference between joy and happiness. Happiness is based on circumstances, while genuine joy is based on Christ. What's more, circumstances can change. Sometimes things are great, and other times they are not. This is why happiness is fleeting. It's a roller coaster of emotion. Yet Jesus, the source of our joy, never changes. "Jesus Christ is the same yesterday and today and forever," says Hebrews 13:8.

Most of us reading this grew up in America—one of the wealthiest and most technologically advanced nations in existence. You would think—since most people believe that money can buy happiness—that we would be some of the happiest people. But look around. Does it look and feel like everyone around you is happy? I don't know exactly how researchers determine these things, but the United States is rarely near the top of the happiness rankings.

Yet we continue to seek after more and more money, thinking it will somehow buy us more happiness. We have the newest smartphones, the most advanced cars, and the latest technological advancements—along with some of the lowest measures of happiness.

The truth is that happiness is the wrong goal. We need Jesus. We need an inner peace, one not based on circumstances but on Christ. He is what will sustain us through the ups and downs of life. We can have true joy when we know we are redeemed, restored, forgiven, and made whole. When we know that our eternity is secure. Romans 8:39 tells us that nothing "will be able to separate us from the love of God in Christ Jesus our Lord." This is remarkable! Imagine waking up and knowing God has a wonderful plan for your life, not just today but every single day. That's because God is sovereign. He's the one who is in control.

JOY AMID TRIALS

James was the half brother of Jesus. (This is not the same James who was the brother of John and one of the original twelve disciples. This other James grew up in the same household as Jesus.) Jesus and James both had Mary as their mother, but James's father was Joseph, while Jesus' Father was God—through the Incarnation, Jesus is God in human form. That's why we say that Jesus is both fully man and fully God.

Now, James had grown up around Jesus, so let me ask you: What would it take to convince your brother that you are, in fact, the Messiah? I mean, seriously! Many scholars believe that this James, Jesus' half brother, did not become a Christ-follower until after Jesus was crucified and then resurrected. While it's hard to say exactly when it happened, at some point James committed his life to recognizing Jesus, his half brother, as the Savior of the world. James even became a leader in the early church. He went through a lot of challenges and suffering for the name of Jesus, and he was ultimately killed for his faith in Christ.

The New Testament book of James is commonly attributed to him, and that's where he wrote this: "Count it all joy, my brothers, when you meet trials of various kinds, for you know that the testing of your faith produces steadfastness. And let steadfastness have its full effect, that you may be perfect and complete, lacking in nothing" (James 1:2-4).

I admit that I have not grown to the point where I "count it all joy" when I go through trials, but I want to. Usually, my first inclination when I am going through a trial is to say, "Help, God—please get me out of this trial!" Or "Where are You, God? Don't You see what I am going through?" Yet I am learning through my struggles to look to God and to realize that He is allowing me to go through them for a reason and a purpose. What is it that He wants me to learn?

I've discovered that it's in these trials that I grow spiritually stronger. It's where I see God do His work. In fact, if you look back over your life, I bet you might say that the hardest times in your life were when you spiritually grew the most. So while I am not there yet, I am learning to face my challenges with joy. I am making an intentional effort to choose joy in the rough times, to remember that God is with me in my struggles, that He is drawing me closer to His heart, and that He is helping me grow in maturity.

We are all on this journey called life, and we all have problems, both big and small. Every one of us has a choice to make each day about what our attitude will be. What attitude will you choose? If you choose joy, you have a greater chance of encouraging those around you. When given the choice, most of us will choose to be around joyful people. When we choose to have the joy of Jesus, others will recognize it. Joy tends to draw people in, and when it does, it has a positive effect on them.

Jesus said, "The thief comes only to steal and kill and destroy. I came that they may have life and have it abundantly" (John 10:10). What Jesus is saying is that we have an enemy who wants to hurt us. Yet we often forget that this spiritual enemy exists, and this is exactly what Satan wants. He is always at work, looking to steal our joy, ruin our relationships, and destroy our lives. Yet our God is greater. Our God *is* God!

Don't let the enemy steal your joy. Make the decision to choose joy in every stage of life. We can become so busy with work, school, kids, and schedules that we neglect to enjoy life. We must schedule time to be with those we love. Pay attention to when your "joy tank" is leaking, and make the effort to refill it. Find those things in life that bring you joy, then choose to invest your time in those things.

If you're a parent, you know there are times you lose your joy. When you first bring home a newborn from the hospital, you are typically filled with joy! But then come the sleepless nights, the continuous cleaning up, and the concerns that come with being responsible for someone else. Everything in your life changes when you become a parent. And as your children grow, there will always be new challenges along the way—busy schedules, financial demands, the craziness of the teenage years! Prioritizing faith and prayer will help you maintain joy in teaching and discipling your family.

HOW TO KEEP YOUR JOY

Some of us have this expectation of life being like what we see on Instagram. Based on social media alone, everyone else seems to have life all figured out. But then we remember that everyone is simply posting their highlights. They post when everything is great, and we end up comparing those images with our struggles. But life is not like Facebook or Instagram. Everyone faces challenges, even if they don't post about them.

That's why one of the best ways to maintain your joy is to manage your expectations. Be realistic about them. Babies cry, couples struggle, and parents grow older, but through it all we can find joy. Don't let the enemy, the devil, steal your joy in life. Don't let him get a foothold in your marriage, your family, your mind, or your heart.

The Bible says, "Do all things without grumbling or disputing" (Philippians 2:14). There are plenty of things in life that try to steal our joy, and complaining is one of them. I know we currently live in a broken and fallen world, but one day everything will be made right! Until then, however, we have to choose joy amid challenges.

In America, of course, we have what are known as "first-world problems." Do you realize that about half the world's people live on less than three dollars a day? Seriously! With that in mind, many of our concerns are not actual *problems* compared with what others face on a daily basis. Almost all of us have (more than) enough food to eat and (too many) clothes to wear. We have homes, cars, families, and friends. Managing our expectations and putting our excesses in perspective can help us choose joy on a daily basis.

Another way to hold on to joy is to enjoy life. I love the word *enjoy* because it has *joy* in it. In his 1908 book *Orthodoxy*, author, philosopher, and Christian apologist G. K. Chesterton wrote, "Joy, which was the small publicity of the pagan, is the gigantic secret of the Christian." That may be true, but we don't have to keep our joy a secret from everyone else. God wants you to enjoy your life. He wants you to live in the moment and have fun. Laugh. Smile. Sing. Christ-followers have a special kind of joy, and it helps move us beyond the ordinary. When we join God in what He is doing, joy bubbles up naturally.

Well-known Christian author C. S. Lewis famously spent many of his younger years as an atheist. When he began teaching at Oxford University, Lewis began hanging around J. R. R. Tolkien and other Christ-followers. There was something different about them. There was a joy and a peace that Lewis didn't have. One day he committed his life to Jesus, and his life was never the same. He went on to become one of the greatest Christian authors and teachers of all time. He wrote *Mere Christianity*, the Chronicles of Narnia series, *The Screwtape Letters*, and many more books and lectures about Christianity. Lewis moved from an ordinary life to an extraordinary one. He titled his memoir *Surprised by Joy*. The events he experienced led to the ultimate joy that came when he committed his life to Christ.

Indeed, Christ-followers should be the most joyful people around. Not only do we have the promise of eternal life, but we truly have everything we need through Jesus. This is how you experience lasting joy: Live your life for Jesus, look to help and serve others, then take care of yourself. Join God in what He is doing, and you, too, will be surprised by joy!

The apostle Paul was imprisoned in Rome for being a Christ-follower, but he didn't let it steal his joy. He knew God was doing something bigger than he could see. He used his time in prison to pray and to share Jesus with his guards. He chose joy over his circumstances. This is different-level joy! In his letter to the church in Philippi, Paul wrote, "I thank my God every time I remember you. In all my prayers for all of you, I always pray with joy because of your partnership in the gospel from the first day until now, being confident of this, that he who began a good work in you will carry it on to completion until the day of Christ Jesus" (Philippians 1:3-6, NIV). Consider his words again: "I always pray with joy . . ." Despite being in prison! Joy comes through Christ and not our circumstances. Joy is recognizing His presence and the blessing of passing on His joy to others.

SHARE JOY

My wife, Lisa, and I came up with the following plan for our kids: When each one turns ten, Lisa takes them on a trip. It's one-on-one time with Mom, but it's also an opportunity for Lisa to talk to them about growing up, how their bodies are changing, and so on. When they reach age twelve, that's when I take them on a trip! We go someplace special that will help them continue to grow and develop. Then, at fifteen, they are allowed to go on their first international mission trip in order to see how the rest of the world lives.

When our oldest daughter, Grace, turned twelve, she wanted to visit Washington, DC. Grace had learned in school about the three branches of government, so she wanted to see the White House, the US Capitol, and the Supreme Court. We arrived in DC on a Sunday evening and stayed with friends while there. We visited amazing museums—the Smithsonian's National Air and Space Museum, National Museum of Natural History, and National Museum of American History, plus the Udvar-Hazy Center at the nearby Dulles International Airport. We had an incredible time laughing and learning together. Some friends even arranged for us to tour the White House.

Grace was in awe. It was definitely an experience she will never forget.

On our trip home, my daughter started to tear up. I asked Grace what was wrong, and she said, "I don't want to share you. When we get home, I will have to share you with my sisters and everyone." The moment was so sweet, and it reminded me how important it is to schedule one-on-one time with our kids.

As parents, the most precious commodity we all have is our time. Yet we don't always use it wisely. Children learn by listening and observing how others live, but I'm not always a great example. I need to be better. The days go by slowly, but the years go by so fast. Our children grow up before we know it, and we never get that time back. I'm speaking to myself when I say that we all need to take time to create experiences and make memories with our kids. It's up to us to take the initiative—to help create joy in their journeys.

As amazing as it was to tour the White House, the best part of our trip—for both of us—was the time we spent together. I want to be a godly follower of Christ, a loving husband, and a great dad, and I want my kids to see those attributes in me. (And I, too, will always remember visiting the West Wing with Grace!)

Since joy comes naturally when you are with those you love, be intentional about scheduling time together. If you are married, when was the last time you went on a date with your spouse? Schedule regular date nights and stick to them!

The dates don't have to be fancy or expensive—simply spending time together (as just the two of you!) is the important part. Also be intentional about your time with your kids. Seriously, put it on the calendar! Whether it's a long-planned family vacation or a spontaneous picnic in the park, both kinds of activities allow you to spend time together. And times together create joy in the journey. They remind you of what's really important.

Speaking of time, you can refill your joy tank by spending time with God. He's the One who brings joy into your life and your heart. I love Psalm 94:19: "When the cares of my heart are many, your consolations cheer my soul." Cheer your soul by spending time with the Lord. Go on a walk or a hike—whatever works for you in order to be alone with God. When you spend time with Him, your joy increases. When you cast your cares on Him, you realize just how much He cares for you (see 1 Peter 5:7).

People often ask me, "How do I know God's will for my life?" I've been asked that question so many times that I've figured out what most people really want to know: How do I know which job to take? What person to date? Where God wants me to live? (We'll dig into these questions later.) Yes, I truly believe God has a unique plan for each person, but as far as the big picture is concerned, God's Word already provides the best instruction: "Rejoice always, pray without ceasing, give thanks in all circumstances; for this is the will of God in Christ Jesus for you" (1 Thessalonians 5:16-18).

"Give thanks in all circumstances." Indeed, your attitude impacts everything. Having an attitude of gratitude is one thing that separates ordinary people from those whose lives have moved beyond the ordinary. Extraordinary people recognize the gifts they have been given, and they make the most of them.

We know from Scripture that God's will for us is to live in joy—always. This doesn't mean we will always be laughing and never experience heartache. It means we will have a joy in our hearts that comes from knowing that God is in control and that He will carry us through any situation or circumstance. The joy of the Lord doesn't show up only when things are going our way, but it also shows up in the difficult times. We can experience joy even in the midst of heartache because we know that our God is always at work for our good and His glory.

GROWING JOY IN YOUR LIFE

When it comes to growing in joy, take note of the root and the fruit in your life. In other words, if you wake up in the morning and immediately *root* yourself in the things of this world, then that will be the *fruit* of your life that day. If you wake up and immediately engage with negative content— whether it's news or politics or social media—then you run the risk of rooting yourself in fear and worry. So if you are struggling with worry, fear, and anxiety, pay attention to how you're starting your day.

It is important to know what is going on in the world, but not necessarily first thing in the morning. If the first thing you do is look at social media, it might be because you're worried about what you are missing out on. "Take every thought captive" (2 Corinthians 10:5) goes right out the window, because you'll be wondering, *Why did they post that? Why was I left out? How can they afford that car or those clothes?* Again, you are rooting your day in worry, fear, anxiety, and envy; therefore, that will likely be the fruit of your day.

Conversely, if you root yourself in God's Word each morning—perhaps via a daily devotional book—and spend some time in prayer, then you should begin to see fruit come out in your life. Peace and patience, for example. The Bible says that "the fruit of the Spirit is love, joy, peace, patience, kindness, goodness, faithfulness, gentleness, self-control" (Galatians 5:22-23). These are some of the attributes that will manifest in your life and bring glory to God. Root yourself in the Lord, and watch how He uses you. A quote most commonly attributed to poet Ralph Waldo Emerson goes like this: "Sow a thought and you reap an action; sow an act and you reap a habit; sow a habit and you reap a character; sow a character and you reap a destiny."

DON'T LET SIN STEAL YOUR JOY

Samson, as described in the Bible, was blessed with incredible strength. Seriously, this guy was a beast. He was filled with the Spirit of God, but he never confronted the sin and lust inside his heart. He was strong on the outside, but not on the inside. He tolerated sin in his life, even when God was doing great things through him. As someone once said, sin takes you further than you want to go, keeps you longer than you want to stay, and costs you more than you ever wanted to pay.

Living an extraordinary life is not just about our outward actions. It's about being willing to master our own hearts and minds, willing to confront the sins inside us. Many people are on the verge of living out their purpose . . . then sin takes them down. Sin destroys. We have an enemy who wars against us. Remember that Jesus said, "The thief comes only to steal and kill and destroy. I came that they may have life and have it abundantly" (John 10:10). You might be thinking, *Why does Satan hate me? What did I ever do to him?* Well, Satan hates God. But Satan knows he can't take down God, so he goes after God's children. God loves you, so Satan wants to destroy what God loves.

So often we tolerate sin. We think we have it under control. We think no one knows about our sin, or we think it's no big deal. But it is a big deal. We think no one knows about the affair. No one knows about the pornography. No one knows about the lust in our hearts and the fantasies in our heads. No one knows about the alcoholism, the anger, the abuse. We think we are skilled at hiding it all, but . . . God knows.

I think about a 1992 incident in which a North Carolina woman called 911 with her free hand because her pet python had swallowed her other hand up to her wrist. By the time help arrived, the twelve-foot snake had coiled around the rest of the woman's arm and started squeezing. Yet the woman immediately told her rescuers: "Don't kill my snake! Don't kill my snake!" What? The snake was trying to consume her! We are often the same way with sin. We think we've got it under control, but all the while it is lurking and will consume us if given the opportunity.

Samson allowed his sin to consume him. He began visiting prostitutes and then became involved with a woman named Delilah (see Judges 16). He kept up the relationship with Delilah even though she tried multiple times to destroy him. Samson just couldn't conquer the sin in his own heart and life. There's no evidence that he ever prayed about it, ever asked for help, or ever sought wise counsel. He just kept living in his sin.

Consider how many politicians, military officers, pastors, teachers, and more have ruined their lives, their families, and their careers over secret sin that was eventually brought to light. It's so sad. They had prominent positions, tremendous opportunities. They had worked hard to build their careers and platforms, only to lose it all. In a moment of passion, anger, drunkenness, rage, or lust, it all fell apart. But in most cases, their downfalls were the result of what had festered in their hearts for years.

What you feed in your heart grows; what you starve dies. If you feed the things of God in your life, then you will grow a heart that is strong, steadfast, godly, and pure. If you feed the things of this world, then that is what will grow in your life. Conversely, if you starve the things of the world—pornography, greed, lust, anger—then they will die out in you.

What are you feeding in your heart?

Samson kept feeding the lust in his heart. He kept going back to Delilah, time and time again. He fought his battles alone, and that never goes well. Eventually Samson gave in and trusted Delilah. He told her the truth about his strength—that God had instructed him not to cut his hair. However, the source of Samson's strength was not his hair, it was God. (Keeping his hair uncut seemed like his *only* act of obedience to God.) Samson told Delilah about this, and she betrayed him to his enemies. They crept in at night and cut Samson's hair. Thus the power of God left him. His enemies took Samson into captivity and even plucked out his eyes. Samson was defeated. His enemies tied him up and mocked him. He was essentially left for dead.

In the end, however, Samson prayed. He turned back to God, and God responded to Samson's cry for help. There were still tremendous consequences for Samson's sin, but I believe he was restored to the Lord in the end.

Don't let sin keep you from all God has for you. Confess your sin and repent. Regardless of who you are or what you have done, when there is God, there is always hope. Call on Him and experience the life that only He can offer. Pray, see a counselor, find some godly people to mentor and encourage you. Don't let the enemy win. Your God is greater. He can forgive, heal, and restore. Trust Him today!

MARTY'S STORY

We recently added a new member to our staff team at church. Marty had been a facilities supervisor at Yale University before he left there to join our team at Rolling Hills. Marty's story is what I call an "only God" story. Marty grew up in Connecticut. He went to church every now and then, but once he was old enough to drive, he never went back. At nineteen years old, Marty joined the army. It was a great fit for him. He loved working with his hands and found a band of brothers. While he was in the army, he married his sweetheart, Maggie.

When 9/11 happened, Marty was a member of the 101st Airborne. His unit was deployed to Afghanistan as part of Operation Enduring Freedom. Next, Marty was sent to Korea. The deployments began to take a toll on him. To cope with the stress, Marty began to engage in online gaming, along with some other unsavory internet browsing. He wanted something, anything, to help him forget about his struggles. To let him escape from the world, even if just for a moment.

After being overseas for almost two years, Marty finally returned home. Coming back was hard. Everything around him seemed to be falling apart. He finally found a job as an electrical apprentice, but Marty's marriage was on the rocks. The coping methods he had brought back with him certainly didn't help. Maggie eventually said she couldn't take it anymore and thought they should call it quits.

Marty was at rock bottom, and rock bottom is where Marty met God. And by His grace, God changed Marty's life forever.

Marty knew he needed help, so he found a counselor to help him deal with his PTSD and his destructive coping methods. He also met a coworker named Ken, who was a Christian, and Ken talked with Marty about the Lord and how to be a godly husband. Marty started listening to Bible teaching on his way into work each day, renewing the ideas that went into his mind and thereby renewing his thoughts. Finally, a friend of Marty and Maggie recognized that their relationship was in trouble and invited the couple to church. So Marty and Maggie went.

After attending church for about six months, Marty and Maggie invited the pastor and his wife over for dinner. For several hours they grilled the pastor with questions: What does it mean to be "saved"? How does one go to heaven? What does God say about marriage? And on and on. That night, Marty lay in bed and prayed, *God, I know You are real. Come into my life. Forgive my sins. I don't deserve it, but I receive what Jesus did for me on the cross. God, I am Yours.* That prayer changed Marty's life forever.

Marty's life was changed, but his circumstances were about to get pretty bumpy. The very next week, Marty and Maggie's dryer blew up and their water heater burst, flooding the basement. Then Marty was the victim of a hit-and-run accident. One night he stood with Maggie in their driveway. She was understandably distraught and angry.

"What are we going to do?" she asked.

"I don't know," Marty said, "but God will provide."

Maggie was blown away. She had never heard him say anything like that. Marty was truly a new man. About a week later, Maggie also gave her life to Jesus.

Today, Marty and Maggie are living their extraordinary lives. They have two wonderful kids. Marty is on our church staff and oversees our multiple campus facilities. He is doing the Lord's work. Marty also co-leads a Bible study for men and attends another. Marty and Maggie have a wonderful home and an infectious joy. They love Jesus, and they are making an awesome impact for His Kingdom. Marty is one of the most joy-filled people you could ever meet.

Our God heals, redeems, and restores broken lives. Our God loves offering hope to all, and He can do the same for you.

WHERE ARE YOU ROOTING YOURSELF?

Take inventory of what you are welcoming into your mind. Are they the things of this world or the things of God? Evaluate how and where you are investing your time, energy, and thoughts. Are the people around you leading you closer to Jesus or further away from Him? Root yourself in the things of God. Apply a spiritual filter to what you watch and read and how you spend your time. What you allow into your mind will ultimately come out in your life.

Remember, if you want joy in the journey, try to root

yourself every day in the Lord. The choice is yours: You can choose to live in fear and worry, or you can choose to live in the promises of God. You can choose to live in negativity, or you can choose to live in joy. Proverbs 3:5-6 says, "Trust in the LORD with all your heart and lean not on your own understanding; in all your ways submit to him, and he will make your paths straight" (NIV). Did you catch that? God wants to guide you! We have a God who is greater and mightier than all the world's leaders. Find Him, and you will find joy in the journey.

7
EVERY DAY MATTERS

Judge each day not by the harvest
you reap but by the seeds you plant.
WILLIAM ARTHUR WARD

CORY SEEMED TO HAVE IT ALL. He spent several years as a pitcher in the major leagues. Only a small fraction of high school athletes ever make it to the professional level, but Cory did it. He retired from baseball at the ripe old age of thirty-two with a wife, a young son, and the rest of his life ahead of him. Cory and his family moved to Middle Tennessee and started attending church. Cory and I went to lunch one day, and he told me, "I feel like there is something missing in my life."

What? From an outside perspective, Cory was living the American dream—a pro athlete career, early retirement, enough money so he would never have to work again, a wonderful wife, a precious son, a gorgeous house, and a dog! What more could he want? It was almost too good to be true, yet Cory told me there was still something missing in his life.

Inside all of us is a need for fulfillment. Money can't satisfy it (though we behave like it can), success in this world cannot satisfy it (though we keep pursuing it), and not even our families or friends can satisfy it (we can't expect ultimate fulfillment via other people—as nice as they might be, they will ultimately let us down in some way). There has to be "something more," and there is.

By God's grace, Cory encountered Jesus and personally committed his life to following Him. It was an incredible, life-transforming moment for Cory. A week before his second child, a daughter, was born, Cory was baptized on Easter Sunday. With family and friends surrounding him, Cory went beneath the water, symbolically dying to his old way of life, and was raised out of the water to walk in a new life with Christ.

As Cory emerged from the water, the place erupted with applause and celebration. Cory's wife and son embraced him—a beautiful picture of true peace and fulfillment. Cory's baptism was just the beginning of his lifelong journey with Jesus. The word *retirement* is not in the Bible, because we never stop following and growing in Christ. Cory joined a men's Bible study, began growing in the Lord, and invited his family in another state to begin watching church online so they could hear more about Jesus.

One day Cory pulled me aside and said he wanted to give me something. Inside the bag he handed me was his jersey from when he had pitched for the Pittsburgh Pirates. I read the note that said, "This jersey is from my first game back after four years of battling surgeries and setbacks. It is the hardest jersey I ever had to earn, and I plan on putting that same effort into my faith."

It has been awesome to see God working in Cory's life. It is by grace that Cory was spiritually saved, and there is this incredible joy in him as he now works out his salvation.

Cory is the spiritual leader of his home. He is a great husband and father. He is active in church. He invites relatives and friends to join his family at church. He even helps mentor underprivileged children. Cory is living his extraordinary life. Being good at baseball is one thing, but being good at life is even more fulfilling. Cory has a personal relationship with Jesus and is living his life for Him. He discovered that every day matters, and he's since found the *extra* in extraordinary living!

WHAT REALLY MATTERS

While some people medicate themselves with addictive substances, others medicate themselves with sports, travel, money, and other pleasures or—in some cases—distractions. While these things are not necessarily all bad, they often dull our senses and rob us of life's real meaning. During the beginning of the COVID-19 pandemic, many communities were under mandatory shelter-in-place restrictions. In our area this lasted for sixty days.

At first, people were shell-shocked. Fear and anxiety were rampant. After a while, however, lots of people began to recognize the things that really matter in life. Sports, travel, and even money were taken away. Many of our usual temporary distractions weren't available. What we *did* have were things with lasting value: God, family, friends, and church community.

I was raised playing sports, and I remain a big sports fan. Growing up in Texas, the Dallas Cowboys were my football team. I watched them, cheered for them, and even allowed defeats to affect my mood—how dare they ever lose! The NFL had a slogan, "Every Sunday Matters." Forget the practices, the preseason, and the press conferences—only the wins and the losses mattered in my young mind.

Sure, sports are exciting, but they don't have lasting value. Cory discovered this, and I have too. I've learned that we can live for the things of God, or we can live for the world. We can grow stronger in our faith and relationships with others, or we can grow weaker by pursuing things that do not last. No longer does every *game* matter; now I know that every *day* matters. Every day we have a God who redeems and restores. Every day we can choose what is best for us and for the people around us, or we can focus instead on our selfish, temporary desires.

As much as I watched and cheered for the Dallas Cowboys back then, I can no longer tell you today how many games they won in a given season, how many points they scored, or even which years they won the Super Bowl. As significant as those details seemed at the time, they ultimately don't matter at all. Sports are great for entertainment and are fun to play, but at the end of the day it's only God, God's Word, and people that truly matter.

POWER IN WORDS

From what you say to others to what you say to yourself, there is great power in words. When I was growing up, there was an old saying: "Sticks and stones may break my bones, but words will never hurt me." We would say that as children, but as we grew up, we realized that this was one of the biggest lies ever told. Long after our cuts and bruises have healed, we still bear the wounds from hurtful words.

I'm guessing that many of you reading this can still remember the painful words a parent, a teacher, a boss, or a coach said to you. We remember the good words, too, but the words that hurt seem to cut deeper and take much longer to fade—if they ever do. Those words still linger in our minds and wreak havoc in our hearts. Words have the power to build up or tear down, and it takes a lot longer to recover from an insult than a compliment.

As a parent, your words carry weight. As a boss, your words carry weight. As a teacher, a roommate, a coworker, or a friend, your words carry weight. Many times we don't realize it—perhaps we are in a hurry, or we are simply not thinking about the effects of what we say—but our words can have a lasting impact.

The Bible puts it this way: "Let no corrupting talk come out of your mouths, but only such as is good for building up, as fits the occasion, that it may give grace to those who hear" (Ephesians 4:29).

How you speak to your children matters.

How you speak to your spouse matters.

How you speak to your friends matters.

How you speak to your coworkers matters.

What if we really paid attention to the words that come out of our mouths? I remember watching a restaurant manager interact with one of his young employees. There was a spill, and the employee did not do a great job cleaning it up. At first the manager responded with a harsh tone, but he looked around, saw me and others, and quickly made a much more polite request to clean the area again. It made me consider how often our words and our tone change when there are other people watching. Yet God is always watching. And the words we say in private can be just as helpful or harmful as any said in public.

Of course, there are times when we need to address an attitude or a situation. There are times as a boss or a parent when you need to do some course correcting. I have always appreciated the "compliment sandwich" approach—first make a compliment, then address the needed behavioral change, and end with another compliment. Studies show that this approach can help maintain the relationship while still addressing the topic at hand.

Let's be the ones who build up those around us. Stop and think before you call, text, write that email, post to social media, or speak to those you love. Slow down and recognize that the person and the relationship are much more important than you being right or even simply heard.

How can you build up those around you this week? Maybe you need to apologize to your spouse, children, roommates, or coworkers for something you said in anger or haste. (Trust me, I have been there.) Ask for their forgiveness, and then move forward in love. "Take every thought captive," the Bible says in 2 Corinthians 10:5—but let's also take *every word* captive. That includes every word we say, type, or text. Remember that we have the power to encourage or tear down. Let's be people who make those around us better. Who can you build up today?

In much the same way, what you say to *yourself* also matters. If you speak or think self-defeating words, then you will live a defeated life. If you keep repeating the wounding words that others said to you, then you will be more likely to live a wounded life. Your words matter. Your thoughts matter. When you speak to yourself in your heart and mind, you need to focus on words of encouragement and truth. You need to tell yourself who you are in Christ: "Therefore, if anyone is in Christ, he is a new creation. The old has passed away; behold, the new has come" (2 Corinthians 5:17). *You* are a new creation. Know it. Speak it.

When you wake each morning, allow the words of your heavenly Father to fill your mind. Changing your thoughts will help change how you live. Instead of being in bondage to old, hurtful words of the past, you will be transformed by new, godly words. You can bless others with your words, and God wants to bless you with His. The battle is first fought in your mind with what you say to yourself. Speak words of hope and life, both to yourself and to others.

YOUR DECISIONS MATTER

Every day you are deciding who you are going to become. I love the biblical story of Josiah. When his father was killed, Josiah became king at the age of only eight. Even at this young age, Josiah decided he was going to live by God's Word. He reigned as king in Judah for thirty-one years. Second Kings 22:2 says, "[Josiah] did what was right in the eyes of the LORD." Every day Josiah chose to follow God. As a result, he was an incredible king who impacted an entire nation.

Conversely, the most disappointing person in history to me is Solomon, a man who had an incredible start. He had a great mother and father, the best education, and a strong relationship with God. Then he became king. Most of us have heard the saying that "with great power comes great responsibility," but Solomon began to drift. Instead of seizing the opportunity to make every day matter, Solomon began pursuing the things of this world. He never renounced God in a big, monumental fashion, but he became enamored of wealth and pleasure in his daily life. Solomon even wrote,

"I denied myself nothing my eyes desired; I refused my heart no pleasure" (Ecclesiastes 2:10, NIV).

And man, was this ever true! For starters, Solomon had some seven hundred wives and three hundred concubines! He might not have turned his back on God or his nation in one fell swoop, but he made decisions day in and day out that progressively led him away from the things that really mattered. At the end of his life, Solomon was worshiping pagan gods; and after he died, the nation of Israel split in two.

The division of Solomon's kingdom is more evidence that our decisions can have an impact far beyond us. We sometimes think, *It's my life. I can do whatever I want.* Or perhaps our attitude is "YOLO!" (You Only Live Once). We often rationalize our poor decisions, but those poor decisions can also come with significant implications for others. Just ask the child whose parent chose to have an affair. Or the employee whose boss chose to mishandle the company finances. Or the passenger in a car with someone who chose to drive while high or drunk. Not only does every decision matter, but every decision can have implications far beyond just our own circumstances.

THE NEXT RIGHT THING

Consciously or subconsciously, we make thousands of decisions every day. Most of them are fairly mundane, but others have serious consequences, and sometimes we simply don't know what to do. So here is a hint when you're facing a tough call: Do the next right thing. Maybe you can't see ahead to the final outcome, but hopefully you can at least see the next step—the next *right* step. The step to pray, the step to trust, the step to have faith, the step to offer grace, the step to forgive. There is always a next step. There's a well-known quote typically attributed to Martin Luther King Jr.: "Take the first step in faith. You don't have to see the whole staircase, just take the first step." The Bible words it like this: "We walk by faith, not by sight" (2 Corinthians 5:7). We can take that next step in faith trusting that God will make things clearer along the way.

There is also wisdom in the old cliché "Take one day at a time." What more can we really do than take each day as it comes—to deal with things as they happen? Why worry about future events that we can't control? The concept is profoundly biblical, as evidenced by Matthew 6:34: "Therefore do not be anxious about tomorrow, for tomorrow will be anxious for itself."

Don't run ahead of God, and don't lag behind. When was Jesus in a hurry? Jesus knew that the Father's plan for His life would be fulfilled at the right time. So often we want to know how the story ends—to skip to the last page and read the conclusion. But resist that urge and take your time. Embrace life and the moments God gives you. Besides, all you can really do is move forward in faith each day, leaving the rest in God's hands. Over time you will see Ephesians 2:10 play out: "For we are his workmanship, created in Christ Jesus for good works, which God prepared beforehand, that we should walk in them." Your life is handcrafted by the grace of our Creator.

I recently had the opportunity to baptize a man in his midthirties who was living proof of this truth. Marcus told me about his life of addiction. Beginning in high school, Marcus was hooked on opioids and alcohol. His life was a constant battle—moving from job to job and relationship to relationship. His life was headed in the wrong direction—fast. Finally, some friends at work intervened. They saw Marcus spiraling downward, and they took him to an AA (Alcoholics Anonymous) meeting where he heard about God. After the meeting, he knew he had a choice to make—a next right step. For Marcus, the next right step was a simple one: coming to the next meeting. Thus began a six-year process of healing and redemption!

As Marcus and I stood in the baptismal water, I could see the transformation on his face and hear it in his story. One day at a time. Each day choosing to follow God, to put himself in a place to succeed, and to live the life God created him to live. The joy of the Lord was evident in Marcus. As his friends, girlfriend, and parents stood nearby and cheered him on, you could see the celebration of many daily steps—six years of choosing to take the *next right step*.

No matter the struggle you are facing, by the grace of God you can win. I love Philippians 4:13, which says, "I can do all things through him who strengthens me." Choose God each day. Don't try to be the perfect you in one day; simply move toward God each day. Wake up thinking about Him. Hang around other people who are following God. Find a good church home. Put yourself in positions to succeed. If you are in a bad job or a bad relationship, start moving in a different, better direction. Move toward the place you want to be.

A common saying among AA participants is the popular Serenity Prayer, which has helped many people in recovery: "God, grant me the serenity to accept the things I cannot change, courage to change the things I can, and wisdom to know the difference." Several clauses were later added to the original prayer: "Living one day at a time, enjoying one moment at a time, accepting hardship as a pathway to peace; taking, as Jesus did, this sinful world as it is, not as I would have it; trusting that You will make all things right if I surrender to Your will; so that I may be reasonably happy in this life and supremely happy with You forever in the next."

Are you trusting your pathway to Him? Are you moving forward or backward? You are never simply standing still. You are always moving. You are either moving closer to God or moving away from Him. You are either moving closer to your spouse or moving away. This holds true even in your thought life. That's why pornography has such a negative impact on so many lives and marriages today.

When a person decides to look at porn, this decision impacts more than just the individual. Those images remain in a person's mind and can erode their capacity for intimacy. It's easy to trade love for lust. Love is others-centered ("What can I do for you?"). Lust is self-centered ("What can you do for me?"). Love is patient, while lust says, "I must have it now." Love is about the other person. Lust is all about me.

God, in His sovereignty, allows us to become some version

of what we pursue. He gives us the freedom to reach for our full potential—or He allows us to squander our lives. Some may ask, "Why does God allow us to decide?" Well, God loves us unconditionally whether or not we *choose* to love Him in return. That's because it's not genuine love unless the other person has a choice in the matter.

If I forced my wife to love me, then we would not have a wonderful marriage. She would essentially be a slave. A captive. Someone with no choice in the matter. But when she chooses to love me of her own accord, then that love is sweet, deep, and beautiful. I chose to love my wife, and I still choose to love her every day. We honor each other with our choices, and our marriage is strong as a result.

Whatever decisions God has set before you, take life one step at a time. Take the next step forward today. You may not arrive tomorrow, or even a year from now, but you will ultimately arrive in God's timing. Remember that while God is with you and for you, He is also ahead of you. So simply take that right next step today. In fact, today could be the first step on a whole new staircase—one that leads to a whole new life. Don't wait to get moving, because every day matters.

A LIFE-IMPACTING CALL

In 2018, I received an unexpected call from Hawaii. Two of my friends were vacationing there with a group of friends. When I picked up the phone, I made a joke about how they were calling me from the most beautiful place in the world.

"This is not a joke," they said. "This is serious. We all just received messages on our phones that a ballistic missile attack is headed for Hawaii."

I couldn't believe it. "Have you talked to the hotel management?" I asked.

"Yes," they replied. "They told us that everyone has received the message and that we need to return to our rooms or find a bomb shelter."

They were scared. I was stunned.

I took a deep breath and said, "Let me pray for you."

They huddled with their friends back in their hotel room and put the phone in the middle of the group. I prayed for God's protection and for His peace. I thanked God that they all had a relationship with Him and that, if this was their time, they would immediately be with Him. We gave thanks that their eternity was secure in Christ Jesus. But I also prayed—perhaps selfishly because they were my friends and I cared for them very much—that they would all be fine and would have many more years on this earth to live their lives for the glory of God. When I finally said "Amen," everyone remained silent.

By God's grace, everything turned out okay. The state's emergency alert unit had mistakenly sent the warning message during a drill, and the alert went out to everyone in the state. Hawaii officials tried to issue a correction right away, yet it was nearly forty minutes before an update went out to everyone's smartphones. During that time there was a lot of panic, confusion, and angst.

When my friends returned home, they told me how different people had responded. Some panicked and ran around screaming. Others walked to the beach. Most called loved ones to say goodbye in case this really was the end. My friends gathered in their hotel room, called friends, and spent time in prayer. They said that even during the craziest moments, they actually felt God's peace and His presence with them.

How would you have responded? What would you have done in that situation? How would you have behaved if you thought those were your last moments alive? Would you panic, or would you have peace? We might think we have a long time left on this earth, but none of us really know. What we do know is what Jesus said in Luke 12:15, that "one's life does not consist in the abundance of his possessions." Money is not the answer. Things are not the answer. God is the answer.

Remember that only three things are eternal—God, God's Word, and people. I have been in hospital rooms with people taking their final breath. When people know they are about to die, most of them want their family and friends to be with them. They want the people around them to know that they love them. They no longer care about awards or trophies. They don't try to buy just one more car. In addition, they rarely hold on to grudges, instead offering grace to all. They want to pray, sing, and share their final moments with those they love.

One day we will all stand before God. Every one of us. It

will be your final exam, and you can begin preparing now. The most important question on that exam is *Did you receive My Son, Jesus, as your Lord and Savior?* You won't be asked about your parents' faith, your church's faith, or your country's faith, but *your* faith. And that exam might happen before you know it!

With that in mind, what do you believe about Jesus *today*? How would you answer that question *today*? If you've read this far, then you know what the correct answer *is not*. It's not "Well, I was a good person." It's not "Well, I went to church every now and then." It's not "Well, I didn't do anything really bad." The question is not about behaving decently or attending church. Neither is it about *religion*. Instead, it's about a *relationship* with God through His Son, Jesus. Have you truly committed your life to Jesus?

That final exam has a second question, one you can also begin to address today: *What did you do with what I gave you?* Remember that everything we have comes from God in the first place. Are you using everything He has entrusted to you—your resources, your relationships, your education, and more—to build your own kingdom or to further God's Kingdom? Are you generous, kind, loving, and gracious? Are you helping others, praying for others, and making a difference in people's lives for the glory of our great God?

When we stand before God, will we be able to say that we poured into our marriage, children, roommates, classmates, neighbors, and coworkers, as well as those we met along the way? Did we invest in the things that are eternal, or did we get caught up in living for the things of this world?

You can clean your house today, or you can clean it in six months. So many of us know the things we need to do in life, but we keep putting them off. Don't put this off! What is God saying to you right now? What is He saying to you through this book? Don't delay. Make the changes you need to make—make them *today*—and begin living the extraordinary life you were created to live.

Some of your best days are still ahead, but living your extraordinary life will likely require some significant changes. Maybe these changes involve saying no to some things that seem *pretty good*, because deep down you know that they are not the *best* things for you. Maybe you need to move on from some old habits or develop some new habits in order to live your best life. I can't tell you exactly what changes you need to make, but I have a feeling that you already have some ideas. If you don't, just ask God for help and guidance. He wants to lead you along His chosen path for your life.

This is your time, so don't put it off. Start living your extraordinary life now.

8
MIRACLES HAPPEN

*The most incredible thing about miracles
is that they happen.*

G. K. CHESTERTON

I CAN STILL REMEMBER THE DETAILS. It was Saturday morning, January 8, 2000, and I was in my office in downtown Nashville trying to catch up on some work. A good friend called me and said he had two tickets to the NFL playoff game between the Tennessee Titans and the Buffalo Bills. He had a conflict and couldn't attend the game. He asked if I wanted his tickets.

What do you think I said?

The game was about to start. I called my wife, but she couldn't go. So I asked a buddy and we headed off to the game. Since we were already downtown, we walked to the Titans' stadium. The place was packed. People were tailgating everywhere. The music was loud, and we hurried to get inside in order to witness the kickoff with sixty-six thousand of our closest friends.

The game was a back-and-forth contest. The team hadn't made the playoffs in years, and everyone was nervous. Somewhere around halftime, a light rain began to fall. A good friend of mine was sitting in a box up high in the stadium. Somehow he spotted me. He came down and asked if we wanted to join him in the box for the second half. Um, *yes!* We'd be out of the rain and get free food? It wasn't a miracle, but it sure felt like one! Now all we needed was a Titans win.

Late in the game, the Titans scored a field goal to take a 15–13 lead. We were all jumping up and down and feeling great—at least until the Bills began driving the ball down the field. With only sixteen seconds left in the game, the Bills kicked a field goal of their own to go up by one point. It was like all the air went out of the stadium. Everyone was deflated. The game was essentially over.

Or was it?

The Bills kicked off, and what took place became known as the Music City Miracle. With time running out, the Titans received the ball, and we all held our breath. The Titans executed a special play known as the Home Run Throwback, and the ball ended up in the hands of Titans player Kevin Dyson on the other side of the field. Almost all the Buffalo defenders were caught off guard when Dyson got the ball and began to run. From up in the box we could see that the Bills players were too far away to catch him. We all started screaming. Dyson ran to the forty, the thirty, the twenty, the ten . . . touchdown! The Titans won the game as time ran out.

The stadium erupted. We all began hugging strangers, high-fiving everyone we saw. My friend jumped on some bank president who was in the box with us. It was probably the biggest celebration in the history of Nashville. We made our way back downtown with thousands of other fans. The cheering seemed to last for hours.

As great as the victory was, the Music City Miracle was not really a miracle. It was an incredible football play, no doubt, and it launched a playoff run that took the Titans all the way to the Super Bowl that year (there was no storybook ending this time, as the Titans fell short by just one yard on their final play), but there are some things we can learn from it. First, genuine miracles leave people with a sense of awe and wonder. Second, they have a lasting impact on people's lives. There can be short-term jubilation, like with a sports victory, but there is also a feeling of wanting more—of realizing that things can be better.

The lasting impact from that football game, at least in my mind, came in the form of the player who scored that last-second touchdown. Kevin Dyson had a good NFL career, but after he retired, he chose to invest in the next generation. He went back to school and earned his master's degree in education. Today he is the principal at a high school here in Tennessee. He could have sat back and lived off past glories, but instead he kept moving forward and began giving back. Kevin's football play seemed "miraculous," but he's now living his extraordinary life, and that's what leaves me filled with awe and wonder.

Let's revisit the story of Peter and John at the beginning of Acts, this time focusing on the lame man in Acts 3 sitting outside the temple courts. His condition left him unable to work, so every day for years, a family member carried him to a temple gate where he begged people for money as they went in to worship.

One day, as Peter and John were going up to the temple, the lame man asked them for money. "Look at us!" Peter said to him. You can imagine that the guy was just going through his normal routine, so when Peter said this, the Bible tells us that the beggar fixed his eyes on the disciples, expecting to get some money. (Isn't this just like us? We think that money will solve our problems.)

Peter then said to the beggar, "I have no silver and gold, but what I do have I give to you. In the name of Jesus Christ of Nazareth, rise up and walk!" (Acts 3:6). Peter reached down and took the beggar by the hand, and the man got up and walked! He stretched his legs and began to jump around. He couldn't believe it!

A crowd soon assembled. Everyone was in awe. They had walked by this guy for years, and now he was dancing in the streets. The beggar went into the temple with Peter and John, and his life was forever changed. I imagine he was glad that he didn't settle for a bit of money!

Yet there's something else to consider. Jesus had probably walked by this same man several times. After all, Jesus had worshiped at that very temple. So why hadn't Jesus healed him? He easily could have, since Jesus healed a lot of people. But He never healed this beggar. Why not? I imagine that every time Jesus walked by the man, He smiled and thought, *Hang in there. Your time is coming. There is a miracle coming your way. Just hold on.* God's timing is perfect. This man's healing, at this time and through these two men, impacted even more people. This was the beginning of the movement that we now know as the Christian church. God used this miracle for maximum impact.

God is not finished with any of us yet. There have been miracles during our lives, whether we recognized them or not, and there might still be miracles to come. We can put our trust in the things of this world and *hope* they will satisfy us, or we can put our hope in God and *know* He will take care of us. He will meet our needs. And not just the superficial ones, but our deepest longings for help, healing, and hope.

God is a God of miracles, and He can take care of you. In fact, He promises to, over and over again. It may not be in our timing, but it is always in His timing. And His timing is perfect.

MANNA

When the Lord brought His people out of Egypt during the time of Moses, He led them through the desert wilderness to the Promised Land. It was a miracle that they were even allowed to leave Egypt. Why in the world did Pharaoh let an entire nation of slaves walk away? Well, it actually took ten miracles (in the form of plagues). God kept fighting for His people, and Pharaoh eventually realized that he was outmatched. The children of Israel were finally free, but how was God going to sustain so many people in the desert? I mean, what food is available in the desert? Almost nothing.

I have been to Israel multiple times, and I have spent a good amount of time in the same wilderness where the children of Israel wandered. The last time I was there, our guide told us that he could not imagine how anyone could survive even three *days* in this wilderness because of the intense heat and the lack of vegetation and water. The wilderness is immense, yet God took care of His people for over forty years as they wandered in the desert. This *was* a miracle!

How did God provide for all these people? Exodus 16 tells us that every morning, when the people woke up, they found a bread-like substance on the ground. God told each family to gather just enough for one day's use. If they gathered more than a day's worth, then it would spoil and grow moldy. But on Friday, the day before the Sabbath, they needed to gather enough for two days because they were to rest on the Sabbath. Only then would the second day's portion not spoil.

The people did not recognize this bread-like substance. "What is it?" they asked. In Hebrew the word *manna* means "What is it?" so the children of Israel called the substance manna.

For years God provided manna for His people. God

also provided water from rocks and streams in the desert, along with meat for them to eat in the form of quail. In Deuteronomy 29:5, Moses said to God's people, "I have led you forty years in the wilderness. Your clothes have not worn out on you, and your sandals have not worn off your feet." God brought them through the desert and into the Promised Land—"a land flowing with milk and honey" (Exodus 3:8).

I'm confident that the Israelites could hardly wait for milk, honey, fruits, and vegetables after forty years of manna and quail! They should have spent only a few months in the desert, but because they didn't trust and obey God, their wandering lasted forty years. Ever feel like you're stuck in the wilderness? We sometimes look back on our lives and realize that if we had trusted God in a certain situation or relationship, we probably could have saved ourselves a lot of time wandering around. Yet even when we don't do our part, our God is still faithful.

God takes care of us in ways both big and small. He makes sure we have clothes to wear and food to eat—even treats that aren't always good for us! God is so good to us. And we have shoes, sometimes lots of shoes. But don't ever forget where these blessings come from. He is the God who provides.

GOD MEETS NEEDS

When Jesus came on the scene in the New Testament, He began to teach around the Sea of Galilee in Israel. The people's response to His teaching is recorded in Mark 1:27: "And they were all amazed, so that they questioned among themselves, saying, 'What is this? A new teaching with authority! He commands even the unclean spirits, and they obey him.'" News about Jesus spread quickly over the whole region of Galilee. Did you catch that the people in the desert and the people who heard Jesus' teaching responded the same way: "What is this?" Manna. God provides for His people. In the desert He provided physical nourishment, and through Jesus, God provides spiritual nourishment. God nourishes our bodies *and* our souls.

God does wonders for His children—not only to provide for us but also to help us grow deeper in our faith. To help us trust Him more. As He instructed His children, don't hoard the manna, but trust that God will provide anew for you each day. As we read in Lamentations 3:22-23, "The steadfast love of the LORD never ceases; his mercies never come to an end; they are new every morning; great is your faithfulness." Don't just store up for yourself more and more, as the rich fool boasted in one of Jesus' parables: "I will tear down my barns and build larger ones, and there I will store all my grain and my goods" (Luke 12:18). It is not about desiring more of the things of this world, but desiring more of the things of God.

God meets spiritual needs as well as physical ones. God is teaching you and growing you in the process. God wants you to run, jump, and dance. He wants you to respond to His goodness much like the man who was healed—thankful and excited. God wants you to come alive both inside and out. Do you love God, or just His blessings? Ask yourself this question: If all the things of this world were stripped away, would God be enough for you? Because God *will* provide for you. God loves you. Will you fully trust Him today?

A FISH STORY

Every year I travel to the Amazon jungle to lead a pastors' conference with Justice & Mercy International. Pastors come from all over the northwestern part of Brazil, also known as the Amazonas region, and I have fallen in love with these amazing men and women.

The Amazon jungle is everything you might imagine and more. It is massive—almost as large as the United States—and the Amazon River makes the Mississippi River look small. There are mesmerizing sunsets, stars, and wildlife. The area is rich with enormous trees, pink dolphins, piranhas, jaguars, sloths, snakes, and so many other amazing creatures. There are things living in the Amazon jungle that can be found only there. Because of its lush vegetation, this part of the world has been referred to as "the lungs of the earth."

Milton is one of the staff team members with Justice & Mercy Amazon. He is also an official jungle guide. Milton grew up in the jungle and knows almost everything about it. In fact, a Russian TV network films a show like the old Discovery Channel series *Man vs. Wild*, and Milton is their "Man."

Milton takes us on jungle walks each year, and I am so glad to be with him. I've watched him reach into an ant nest and smear ants all over his body as "insect repellent." He's shown us which plants are safe to eat and which ones are deadly. I've seen him dive into the Amazon River at night and come out of the water with a baby caiman (a small, alligator-like reptile) for us to hold. He can grab an anaconda by the tail and walk up to its head in order to get control of it. No way would I ever try this stuff, but somehow I feel safer when Milton is around.

Millions of people live in the Amazon basin, so when God says in Acts 1:8 that "you will be my witnesses in Jerusalem . . . and to the end of the earth," this feels like it. There are some bigger cities along the Amazon's shores, but there are also villages that have rarely, if ever, seen an outsider. It is an incredible place that I have grown to love.

Through Justice & Mercy Amazon, we host two pastors' conferences each year in the jungle. We operate a conference center located about three hours by boat down the river from Manaus, Brazil. Pastors come to our conferences from all over the jungle—hundreds of pastors and their wives every year. This is the only training and even the only vacation time that many of them receive during the year. (Let that sink in for a minute.) They are excited to be there, so we try to make the week a special one. I know one pastor who travels nine days by canoe to reach the conference center! All these pastors are inspiring, and so are their stories.

Mike Minter, longtime pastor of Reston Bible Church in Washington, DC, helped launch the conferences about ten years ago. "We go to teach them theology," Mike says, "and they teach us about Jesus." (You can read more about these conferences in my book *Immeasurably More*, as well as in *Wherever the River Runs* by Kelly Minter, Mike's daughter.)

When you have only the Lord to depend on, then you know it is He who answers your prayers. We sometimes lose sight of God's wonders today because we are surrounded by so many distractions. *Did God provide that job for me, or was it LinkedIn? Did God heal the family member I prayed for, or was it the doctors? Did God provide the protection I asked for, or was it the police?* You see, I believe God uses all these things—including job placement services, doctors, and law enforcement—to accomplish His plans and work wonders in our lives. But sometimes we attribute the glory that belongs to Him to the wrong person or place. Sometimes we praise the people and things that God uses instead of the One who provided them in the first place.

In the Amazon, however, there are rarely such distractions. When you are in need, in trouble, or afraid, often the only thing to do is to pray. The people who live there see God work wonders up close. Their stories, and their lives, continue to move me. We have heard miraculous stories of people raised from the dead, enemies whose weapons won't fire, deadly animals turning away from villages, and flood waters receding. These stories seem impossible apart from the power of God's hand and the power of prayer. They are miraculous instances of God taking care of His people.

One of my favorite stories is that of a young pastor and his wife. Floodwaters had ruined their crops and left them and their children without food. They prayed about their situation as a family and then went to church. At church they learned of a widow in need in another village. After the church service, they decided to go help this widow. But the pastor's wife did not want to go. She told her husband that they needed to go home and start fishing in order to have food for their family.

"God will provide," replied the pastor.

On their way back home from helping the widow, in the middle of the Amazon River, a fish jumped into their canoe. Literally jumped right in! The wife screamed, and the pastor jumped on top of it. It was a large fish—enough to feed their family for two weeks. And it was not just any old fish—it was a delicacy! This type of fish was sold at the market in Manaus for a premium. God had provided!

God invites each of us to watch Him work. God's provision is not reserved just for pastors or for people in the Bible. God works wonders today. God works through His people— people like you. You can help someone else. You can sponsor a child in need through Justice & Mercy International, Compassion International, or World Vision. You can do ministry work in your community or through your church. You can help feed the hungry in your city. We can't do it all alone, but we can all do something. We can all help make a difference.

You never know where God will take you when you accept His invitation to act, but you can trust that there will be joy and life-changing moments. He can help you see and do things you never imagined. You can witness lives saved and changed in the process.

I know many people in the United States who have been blessed, and they, in turn, want to bless others. Many of these people have gone on international mission trips to serve the underserved around the world. Others support orphaned or otherwise vulnerable children right here in America. Through these efforts, countless children have received food and clothing, furthered their education, and secured jobs.

I have had the privilege to walk young women—girls who we supported as children—down the aisle at their wedding. It is incredible that God would allow us to participate in these holy, life-impacting moments. Some people I know have even helped orphaned children find forever families in the United States. It's amazing to me that God allows us to help provide an answer to someone else's prayer.

We have young adults in our church who grew up in orphanages in Moldova. By God's grace and the generosity of God's people, they have been able to come to America. They have been able to study here, secure jobs, start families, and thrive. Every time I see them, I am reminded of God's grace—even in my own life. I see their young children and think about future generations growing up with hope, joy, and love.

Our call as Christ-followers is not to make as much money as we can just so we can retire early, go sit on some beach, and drink fruity drinks. Retirement is not our goal—Jesus is our goal. Sitting home alone is not our goal—making a difference in this world is our goal. Let's not waste our days. Let's not be ordinary. Eternity matters, and lives are at stake. This is our time and our opportunity. Let's be extraordinary!

GOD PROVIDES

I realize that most of us are not riding in a canoe on the Amazon or working in an orphanage in Moldova. But we all face challenges and struggles wherein we need God to show up in our lives. A good friend named Dwayne told me about the early years of his marriage, when he and his wife had two small children and a lot of expenses. One day Dwayne's wife began experiencing serious pain in her body. They went to the emergency room at Vanderbilt University Medical Center, and she was admitted. They were scared and both began to call out to God.

The doctors ran some tests and told them that Dwayne's wife had cancer. It's the word we all fear, and it shook them to the core. The doctors said she would need surgery immediately. Dwayne and his wife looked at each other in disbelief. They held hands as they waited for a visit from the surgeon. Here they were, a young married couple with children. And because my friend was a musician, they didn't have any health insurance. How would they ever make it?

Dwayne was worried, first and foremost for his wife, but also for their finances. He knew that the treatment could potentially cost hundreds of thousands of dollars—an amount that could put them in debt for the rest of their lives.

There was so much fear, so much unknown. What was going to happen? Dwayne prayed like he'd never prayed before. And that's when the surgeon entered their hospital room.

The surgeon told Dwayne and his wife about the procedure and the expected recovery time. The surgeon was blunt—it would be a very invasive surgery that would take a long time and carried a high risk. They needed to know how serious the situation was. After they spoke, Dwayne finally asked, "Doc, we don't have insurance. How much will all this cost us?"

"Well," the doctor replied, "I am going on vacation after this surgery, so I am going to do this one for free. It is on me. You will still have the hospital bills, but don't worry about this surgery."

Dwayne was in shock. He says it was at this point that he knew for certain: God was with them.

By God's grace the surgery went great. But the hospital bills still loomed. Even as Dwayne celebrated his wife's recovery, he always knew in the back of his mind that the hospital bills were coming. And come they did. He received a bill for several thousand dollars a few months after the surgery. How were they going to pay?

After much anxiety and prayer, Dwayne finally got up the courage to ask the hospital about a payment plan. He hoped they would let him pay it off over the years to come. The person who answered the phone asked for his account number. Dwayne gave it to them, they put it into the system, then they asked for it again. He gave it again. Then came the response.

"Sir, your bill has been paid. Someone came in this morning and paid your entire bill. In fact, they overpaid by a little, so we will be sending you a check."

What? Only God! Dwayne began to sob, then gave all the glory to God.

Today Dwayne's wife is cancer free. She herself is a wonder—an amazing wife and mother. Our God is still at work. We simply need to open our eyes and hearts to see, to receive, and to give Him the glory. God is constantly providing for us, but how often do we stop to think about how we have food, clothing, jobs, family, or friends? Where did all this come from in the first place? It's because God provides. It's because God sustains. And if He has promised to take care of us, then why do we continue to worry? God's got this.

Maybe you are in desperate need right now. Don't stress or lose hope. Pray and give your circumstances over to God. Trust that He has the best for you. Do the next right thing. As I've said before, trusting God doesn't mean things will always work out exactly how you want them to, but you can believe that God loves you and wants the best for you. Trust Him. Whether your need is financial, relational, or spiritual, God can provide. Who knows—a fish might even jump into *your* boat today!

9

DISCOVER
your PASSION

*Nothing great was ever achieved
without enthusiasm.*

SAMUEL TAYLOR COLERIDGE

LIVING IN NASHVILLE, I know a lot of people pursuing a career in music. You meet some of the most gifted singers, musicians, and songwriters in the world here in Nashville. Everyone has a story. Take my good friend Kelly Minter, who came to Nashville to pursue music. She left her home, her family, her friends, and everything she knew to pursue her passion. She was bold. She went for it. And she is good. Kelly is a talented songwriter, singer, and guitarist, and she has a great stage presence.

After being here for a while, Kelly began to realize how hard it is to make it in the music industry. Some other job opportunities came up, so she took them to help make ends meet. Yet Kelly kept pursuing her passion. She didn't let the other jobs snuff out the desire inside her. She did not get distracted. It was difficult, but in the process, God was refining Kelly's passion for Him. God was molding her into the woman He had created her to be. Her anxiety about not "making it" began to give way to an even deeper faith and trust in God.

One of Kelly's songs eventually began to get some traction. She recorded an album and was picked up by a record label. She thought her passion was simply to perform on a stage, but she began to recognize that her deeper passion was to share God's love with others and to help women grow deeper in their faith. She began writing Bible studies along with her songs—and people responded.

Today, Kelly Minter is one of the leading women's Bible study authors in our country. She travels all over the world teaching the Bible and—get this—playing her songs! In arenas, at churches, and on stages, Kelly shares her music and her heart with others.

I'm thankful that Kelly did not settle. She took on extra work when she needed to, but she kept pursuing her life's passion. She did not allow money to become her goal. If God wants you to follow your passion, then He will provide.

Kelly is an amazing writer, author, and musician. I encourage you to pick up one of her Bible studies—and when you do, thank God that she did not give up on her dream or settle in just any job. She is using the gifts and talents that God put inside her.

Scripture says, "Delight yourself in the LORD, and he will give you the desires of your heart" (Psalm 37:4). What a promise! Note that the second part is based on the first. God will give you the desires of your heart *when* you get to the place where you delight in Him and His Word. When you make Jesus a priority. When you seek after His presence. When you care more about knowing what He has to say than anyone else. It's then that your desires become more God-focused—more about Him than you. The Lord wants you to discover your God-given passions, and He wants to bring to life those desires that He's placed in your heart. Begin to move in that direction.

Ask yourself (and God!) what steps you can take to discover your God-given passions. Maybe reading a book, watching a video, or listening to a podcast can help you determine the gifts and talents inside you. Maybe it begins with making contact with someone in a particular field who can help you. It might even involve setting aside time and money so you can invest in your dream.

Now, I'm not suggesting that you immediately quit your job and go in a whole different career direction. (Seek wise counsel before you make any drastic moves!) More often it's better to simply be intentional, to do *something* each day that moves you forward. Change the trajectory of your life, even one degree, and you will change your destination.

Maybe your passion is to be a good mother to your children. Then be the best mom you can be! Do something each day to bless your kids. (They grow up fast, so don't put it off!)

Maybe write notes to put in their lunch boxes. Maybe say a special prayer together every night. Maybe take an occasional day trip for some one-on-one time. Just try to do something intentional as regularly as possible.

Maybe your passion is to start a business. Connect with someone who has started their own successful business. Develop contacts in that field and ask them questions. Take some business classes, either in person or online. Most of the time, the hardest part is just getting started. You certainly don't have to quit your current job right away, but you do have to be intentional about exploring the process.

Maybe your passion is to help others. Look for opportunities in your community or through your church. Instead of streaming the latest shows, take some time each day to learn what needs are out there. Ask God to lead you and guide you to the right people and the right opportunities.

Your passion doesn't have to be glamorous or all-consuming. You can still have time for your family, your job, and your friends. You simply need to prioritize the time you have and focus on what really matters. Living your passion changes you. When you explore your passion, you feel more alive. It gives you joy. You wake up excited, and you look forward to the day ahead.

When you are fulfilled in life, you are a pleasure to be around. Your loved ones will appreciate you more. Your spouse will appreciate you more. Your kids might even appreciate you more. We think our kids want stuff, so we work overtime to give them things that they don't even use a year later. But your kids want *you*! They want you fully engaged. And this happens when you are living your passion.

If you are not yet living your passion, then now is the time to act. Don't settle for where you are in life today. Move forward. Move toward becoming the man or woman God created you to be. Live with tenacity. Pursuing your life's passion is not always easy, but it is worth it. Remember that if you delight in God, then He will give you the desires of your heart.

Just as God made you unique physically, God also created you with unique dreams, goals, and passions. Some people, like me, are extroverts. The more people around me, the better I feel. I am energized by people. Others, like my wife, are introverts. Give her a night at home with her family—in her pajamas—and you will see a happy woman.

The point is that we all are wired differently, and we all have different talents and passions. Some people light up like a Christmas tree when they talk about serving or traveling or fishing. What lights you up? You might not be able to make a career out of fishing—though a few do!—but try to make some time for what gives you joy.

I believe that our passions come from God. He knows how you work. He knows what invigorates you and inspires you. He also knows what drains you and exhausts you. People who spend their lives living outside their passion often feel tired, run down, and even trapped. They know there has to be more to life, but they can't put their finger on it. There is this longing inside them.

Whether we ignore our longings, cover them up, or medicate them, the truth is that we are not fulfilled, so we try anything and everything to take our minds off the feelings of dissatisfaction. Maybe it starts with a glass of wine, then another, and another. You go on a vacation, and on the way home you are already thinking about the next trip. You attend a concert or sporting event and want to linger around afterward so you don't have to return to your "normal" life.

There are plenty of people who are just not happy. They are always complaining, always frustrated, always down on themselves and everyone around them. Do you know people like this? Are you one of these people? Do you always have something to complain about? Maybe you have a boss or a coworker or a classmate you don't like. Perhaps the root problem is that you have not yet found your passion.

Maybe you have a job that pays decent money, but you hate the work. Keep in mind that when you are not happy with your life, those negative feelings often affect the people around you. People complain about their spouse or their kids or their coworkers—but the real problem is not with all those other people; the problem is with *them*. When you are not content and fulfilled in life, you may end up taking out your frustration on others.

But what if you *could* live your passions? What if you woke up every day with joy? What if you bounced out of bed ready to embrace the day with enthusiasm? The word *enthusiasm* comes from two root words: *en*, which translates as "in," and *theos*, which means "God." This reminds me that enthusiasm comes from living "in God." When we are pursuing our God-given passions, the everyday hurts and frustrations in life don't seem like a big deal anymore.

Your challenge is to discover your passion—what makes you feel alive. Make this task a priority.

So how do you do that? I'm glad you asked. As always, the process starts with God, and it starts with your heart. Is God on the throne of your heart, or have you let the desires of the world consume you? Are you more interested in receiving the applause of man than you are in receiving the favor of God?

When you live for others' approval, you will often find yourself in debt. You spend money to impress people, so you overspend on things like cars and houses. When you live to impress, you spend time on social media comparing yourself with everyone else. You feel like you are falling behind because other people have more or better than you. Well, stop it! Stop the madness. Get off the carousel of comparison and put God first in your life.

Then take time to *ask* God. Seriously, have you ever prayed about your passions? God made you, so He knows. James 1:5 says, "If any of you lacks wisdom, let him ask God, who gives generously to all without reproach, and it will be given him." Spend time in prayer, ask Him about your dreams and desires, and commit to living each day for Him. Then search your heart. You know deep down how God wired you. You know what you love to do. (One caution here: You might love to sing, yet you can't carry a tune in a bucket. Simply put, if God wanted you to be a performing artist, He would have given you the talent for it.)

Ask yourself, *What would I do if money weren't an object?* So often we take a job based on the salary, and many times we do need the money. That's okay for a season, but when we stick with a job *only* for the money, then sometimes money becomes our passion. I believe that none of us are wired just to make money. When that's our focus, we can remain in a job we hate for *years*.

We might be miserable in our situation, but now our spending has increased to the point that we need the money from this job we hate just to support our new lifestyle. What we really need now is not more money, but rather a change in our thinking. That change might involve small steps or big ones, but the goal is to stop doing what makes us miserable. Those steps might include budgeting and cutting back on our lifestyle, finding opportunities to volunteer, developing our prayer life, pursuing our passions in the evenings, or all the above. You are *not* simply stuck where you are. Look for ways to move in the direction of your heart. Change your thinking, and you change your life.

ASK OTHERS

Another step involves asking others. If you're not sure what your passion is, ask people what they see in you. We all need wise people in our lives. Listen to the people who know you best, the people you trust. Talk to your friends, your spouse, your coworkers, or your pastor. What do they see in you? How and when do they see you most alive and energized? Consider a move in that direction. God uses others to speak into our lives. I love Proverbs 27:17: "Iron sharpens iron, and one man sharpens another." Who are you allowing to sharpen you?

Many times, your passion might not work as a career. In that case, your job may provide the financial stability you need while you endeavor to fulfill your passion.

After you've asked those around you, next ask yourself:

- *What do I love?*
- *Do I have time to volunteer?*
- *Can I fulfill my passion on a part-time basis?*

If you are married, share your feelings with your spouse. Can you work together to help you both fulfill your dreams? Be honest and open with each other, as this can strengthen and grow your marriage. Talk about how you can take steps toward your goal that don't involve quitting your job and just hoping for the best. Pray with your spouse and brainstorm ways to make life changes that you both are comfortable with. Maybe it's time to work on your resume, or to dust off that old business plan and look at it with fresh eyes.

If you are single, maybe reach out to a pastor or godly friend for advice. If you are a teenager, talk to your parents or with a mentor at church or school. Consider taking an aptitude test to see what your strengths are, then use that in conjunction with exploring what you love to do. Consult with people who really know you as you assess what fills up your heart.

Will you discover and fulfill your life's purpose? You only get one shot at life, so don't settle for the ho-hum, the benign, the okay. No one else was created just like you, so pursue your passion. I believe in you. God believes in you. Every day take another step forward. You will be glad you did.

THE PASSION OF BEING LIKE JESUS

The Bible encourages us to emulate Jesus. God wants us to be "conformed to the image of his Son" (see Romans 8:29). This is God's plan for you—not only what job you do, or what family you belong to, but also how the entirety of your life is shaped.

Speaking of how lives are shaped, allow me to tell the story of John Pac.

I hinted at John's story in the introduction of this book. And for those of you who've read my book *Immeasurably More*, I included it there as well. If you aren't familiar with his story, let me recount it again.

John Paculabo—or John Pac, as most people call him—is one of the most remarkable people I've ever known. Born and raised in England, John gave his life to the Lord at an evangelistic event when he was eighteen. At the time he had two loves—soccer and music. John was part of a folk band that was birthed out of the church he attended with two of his friends. They performed at both mainstream and Christian festivals, plus at events throughout the UK and Europe. After God captured his heart, John began to wonder what life was really about.

God never wastes any talents He wants to use, and God began to use John's love for music. He went from being part of a band to producing music for other Christian artists. John joined Kingsway Music and eventually became the company's managing director. He was known as one of the founding fathers of the British Christian music scene, introducing listeners to artists and songwriters such as Matt Redman and Stuart Townend. God used the music that John and Kingsway produced to bring a revival through worship to the global church.

When John was in his fifties, he said to his wife, Juliet, "We should buy a villa in Spain. We could spend half the year in Spain and the other half in England." That same year, John went on a fishing trip to the Amazon. (After all, every great fisherman wants to catch a peacock bass—and the Amazon River is home to the peacock bass, along with some of the best fishing in the world.)

As John was traveling along the Amazon in a fishing boat, he noticed an old, run-down building with kids gathered all around and in it. It was over one hundred degrees outside, so John wondered what the building could be. He leaned over to his guide.

"What is that?" he asked.

"That is a school," came the response.

John looked again, and he immediately thought, *That can't be a school. There is no way. Something must be done to help these children.* That very night, John called back home to Juliet in England. "We are going to build a school in the Amazon," he told her. "I don't know how, but we are going to do it." He later took Juliet to the Amazon to see for herself. Needless to say, she was all in.

Over the next seven years, John and Juliet worked with some board members of Kingsway Music and others in Brazil to build twelve schools in villages along the banks of the Amazon. They also spent more than $1 million on a community center for training pastors and teachers and for distributing vital supplies. John bought a boat, the *Discovery*, to transport mission teams to serve in the villages. John often spoke of his love for the Amazon people, and he took many to see the work God was doing in the jungle.

At the beginning of this chapter, I mentioned my friend Kelly Minter, who has recorded with Kingsway Music. John invited Kelly on one of the Amazon mission trips, and Kelly invited a friend of hers, Mary Katharine Hunt, to accompany her. At the last minute Kelly couldn't go, but Mary Katharine went anyway. When Mary Katharine returned, she was so moved by the need, the ministry, and the reception she had received from the local people that she asked if our church, Rolling Hills, and JMI (Justice & Mercy International) would like to get involved with the ministry there.

After about two years of ministry together, I received news

that John Pac had been diagnosed with stomach cancer. John asked if a few of us could fly to England and meet with him because he was no longer able to travel. When we landed, we received a message to hurry to John's home.

We found John in a hospital bed in the middle of his living room. His entire family—Juliet, kids, and grandkids—were present, along with the board of Kingsway Music. John was on oxygen, but he was completely coherent. He welcomed us, introduced everyone, and then announced that he wanted the last thing he did on this earth to be for the poor and the forgotten in the name of Jesus. For the next four hours, John spent time transferring all his assets in the Amazon over to JMI. We prayed and sang together, then John said he was tired and closed his eyes. We returned to our hotels, and I remained in awe of the beauty and generosity I'd just witnessed.

The next day we returned to see John. We could sense that something was happening. John looked at Juliet and said, "I love you," then closed his eyes and went home to be with Jesus. What an incredible man of God, and what a life and legacy!

From that day forward, the ministry that John began in the Amazon has continued to thrive. Today we host multiple pastors' conferences at the John Pac Center, impacting hundreds of ministers from all over the Amazon region. These pastors take the gospel "to the end of the earth" (Acts 1:8). We have built several more schools and have a full-time staff in the Amazon to help run the ministry, mission trips, libraries for teaching literacy, and a medical ministry to numerous villages in the region.

John's daughter Lucy moved from the UK to the United States and is now working full-time with Justice & Mercy International. She is carrying on her father's legacy to the poor and forgotten. In addition, Mary Katharine Hunt left a high-paying executive job in Nashville to become the executive director of Justice & Mercy International, and she now leads both the work with orphaned and vulnerable children in Moldova and our ministry to the poor and forgotten in the Amazon. Thanks to John Pac's commitment to Christ and the passion he discovered in the jungles of the Amazon, the Good News is impacting countless people today.

"I wasted so much time on trivial things," John once said, and I will never forget his next words: "I just wish I had gotten it sooner." His love for God, his commitment to the poor, and his desire to invest in ministry have outlasted him and have resulted in lasting impact for the Kingdom. John's passion and influence live on.

Don't spend your time wishing that you had gotten it sooner. Wherever you are now, today, begin living your extraordinary life. Like John, we can get caught up in the trivial, but our obedience to God is what matters. God wants to use all of us to help make a difference. Let's start now.

10

FAITH
over FEAR

*Never be afraid to trust
an unknown future to a known God.*

CORRIE TEN BOOM

MIKE FISHER WAS BORN AND RAISED in Canada. He grew up going to church with his parents, and for many years he was growing in his faith and making good decisions. Like many other Canadian boys, Mike loved ice hockey. What's more, he was *really* good at it.

Mike achieved his childhood dream at age eighteen when he was drafted into the NHL. He signed a big-time contract with the Ottawa Senators. By age nineteen Mike had gained everything he thought he wanted—he was playing professional sports and enjoying all the fame and fortune that came with it. But while he was living his dream, Mike still felt empty inside. Something was missing.

God gently tugged at Mike's heart for five years, and his life made a 180-degree turn at age twenty-three when he showed up at a cousin's Bible study. The Scripture they read that day was Luke 9:25, where Jesus said, "What good is it for someone to gain the whole world, and yet lose or forfeit their very self?" (NIV). That's when Mike realized that while he had gained what the world had to offer, he was still losing his soul. Right then and there, Mike committed his life to following Jesus. He was baptized soon after, and his new life in Christ began.

Mike's journey of faith included giving back to the needy in his community. He also decided to avoid dating until he met the kind of girl he would ultimately marry. Mike prayed for a godly woman, and he eventually met country music star and *American Idol* winner Carrie Underwood. Mike knew that God had answered his prayers in bringing the two of them together. Their relationship was a special one, and they were married in 2010. They are an exceptional couple—Mike Fisher, the beloved NHL hockey player, and Carrie Underwood, the award-winning country music singer.

After the couple were apart for long periods while Mike played hockey for the Senators and Carrie pursued music in Nashville, God opened the door for Mike to be traded to the Nashville Predators. Mike retired from professional hockey in 2018, and he and Carrie have two wonderful sons, a beautiful home, and lots of godly friends and family.

Their journey together has been amazing, and it's not over

yet. But things could have been very different if Mike had ignored the tugging in his heart and settled for the world's plan for his life, or even his own plans. God's plans are always better than we can imagine. I am sure Mike would agree that he is extremely pleased that he sought out God's plan for his life.

It's not every day that a professional hockey player acknowledges his need for God and is baptized at the age of twenty-three. It takes courage. But what a difference God makes when we step out in faith and follow Him!

Fear is one of the biggest deterrents to truly living an extraordinary life. We all struggle with fear at times. Maybe you were afraid to try out for the soccer team or the school play, and today you still wonder if you would have made it—or if you would have been any good! Perhaps you're afraid to apply for your dream job because you're not sure you're good enough. We're even afraid to ask for forgiveness because we're not sure if we'll receive it. Fear can paralyze us and keep us from reaching our full potential. It can also keep us from following the voice of God.

We all make choices regarding how we'll live each day. Will we live in faith or in fear? An encouragement to resist fear appears 365 times in the Bible—once for each day of the year! Do you think God is trying to make a point? I do. If we truly believe that God is with us and for us, then that belief should impact how we live. If we truly believe that God, our heavenly Father, will take care of us, then that belief should impact how we make decisions. He is God, and we are not. Furthermore, He is faithful. Because of this, we can live in faith and not in fear.

When God calls you to be bold, be bold. Don't make excuses. It's normal to prefer the safe and comfortable, but God wants us to live lives of adventure. God wants us to "come, follow" Him (Matthew 4:19, NIV). Does following Jesus involve risk? Of course it does! But it's a no-lose proposition from an eternal perspective. So many of us are afraid of failure, but the only lasting failure is to not follow the Lord.

Remember this: God is with you, and He is for you. First John 4:18 says, "There is no fear in love, but perfect love casts out fear." As you look to Jesus, you see perfect love. As you hear what He says about you, you experience His peace. As you trust the perfect love of God, your fears recede and eventually fade away. God has your best interests in mind.

Where is your faith today? When you look at your life, do you see chaos or calm? Do you get caught up in the hustle and bustle, or do you rest in the peace that God offers? My prayer for you is that you will experience the genuine peace of God. In times of laughter and in times of pain, I pray you will experience the promise of Philippians 4:7: "And the peace of God, which surpasses all understanding, will guard your hearts and your minds in Christ Jesus."

Whether or not you are where you want to be in life, take comfort in knowing that God is with you. Maybe there is a missing relationship in your life—remember that God is with you. Maybe you feel out of control. If so, look to the One who is in complete control and hear Him say, "Do not be afraid." His words bring peace.

Jesus said, "In the world you will have tribulation. But take heart; I have overcome the world" (John 16:33). There are real challenges that we all face in life. In fact, Jesus *promised* us that these challenges would come! We can choose to face them alone, or we can choose to face them with the help of our great God. We can choose to move forward in faith and watch God do what only He can do.

I love what Paul wrote to a young man named Timothy: "For God has not given us a spirit of fearfulness, but one of power, love, and sound judgment" (2 Timothy 1:7, HCSB). Are you living by fear or by faith? Are you being bold when God calls you to help someone, to pray, to get involved, or to initiate a spiritual conversation? What is your first response? As we mature in our walk with God, we will become bolder, both in faith and in serving others.

HIKING THE NARROWS

Several years ago we took a family vacation to Zion National Park. I might be biased, but I think this park is one of the most beautiful places in the world. My family loves to hike, and there are all kinds of amazing trails in the park. But we had heard about one particular trail called The Narrows.

Some friends first told us about this hike, so we looked

online to learn more. The route, we discovered, takes hikers through a river and into a stunningly beautiful canyon with sheer mountains on both sides. Everything we saw and read said it was spectacular, but it would not be easy. At some points we would literally be walking through the river. Yet the photos looked awesome, so we decided to go for it.

We woke up around four thirty in the morning to rent the equipment for our hike. Everyone told us we needed waterproof boots and special socks, as well as walking sticks. After renting our equipment, we caught an early shuttle to the park. We wanted to see the sunrise, so we were some of the first people to arrive. The sun was coming up as we approached the trailhead, and we could already see the beauty of this majestic area.

There were a lot of people on the trail that day. Families with small children, couples, younger and older people alike. It's quite a popular trail. When we came to the river, at first it was only ankle deep. As we began pressing farther along, the crowd started to thin. Several folks turned around after a couple of hours and as the water got deeper.

After about three hours of crossing and recrossing the river, we noticed that the mountains on both sides began to narrow and the only available path was in the water. More people turned around at this point. There are some big stones in the river on each side, so we found ourselves climbing up and over the rocks, trying not to slip. After yet another hour, the water was now up to our knees.

Our three kids were troupers. We asked them if they wanted to turn around. "No," they said. "We want to go to the end." After about another hour, the water was now up to our waists (nearly chest level for our two younger kids, who were twelve and fourteen at the time). We were four hours in, with not many others around by this point. The mountain walls on both sides now reached hundreds of feet into the air, and the view was already sensational. It wasn't easy, but we kept going.

We made it to the end at last, and the view was astounding! It was the most difficult hike of our entire trip, but it's also the one we will most remember. It was as if God took His finger and carved out a narrow flowing river through the mountain. By the time we made it back, we had been outside for over nine hours. We were exhausted, yet full of joy for completing the journey.

People who live extraordinary lives keep going, even when the going gets tough. We know there will be challenges, but the deeper you go, the richer the journey becomes. Struggles make many people stop. Fear makes many people stop. There are always excuses, and sometimes we turn around instead of going forward.

The challenges are real, but the rewards are enormous. You *can* live your extraordinary life.

As you grow deeper in your relationship with God, you often find more and more confidence. The more you fall in love with God, the less fear you experience. When you focus more on what God says about you, you worry less about what someone else says. Fear stops us. Fear keeps us from going forward. Yet God calls us to go forward. God wants us to reach our full potential.

The Bible says, "We walk by faith, not by sight" (2 Corinthians 5:7). Even when we can't see what's ahead, God wants us to go deeper with Him—to pray, to read His Word, to invest our lives in the things that matter. Sometimes it is easier to sit on the couch and watch Netflix or Hulu, but God has so much more in store for us. Keep walking. Keep moving forward. Live by faith and not by fear.

We first discussed "next steps" in chapter 2. Let me challenge you again: What next step is God calling you to take in your faith journey? Is there something God has put on your mind and heart to do? Maybe it's forgiving someone. This can be a big step, as well as an opportunity for you to trust God. Maybe it's maintaining your devotion to God's Word and prayer. Maybe it's attending a church or finding a community of godly friends. Maybe it's committing your life to following Jesus. Maybe it's being baptized and making a public commitment to Christ. All I know is that when you put your faith in Jesus, your fears begin to fade. Whatever is making you fearful today, turn it over to the One who cares about you. The water might be getting deeper, but our God is with you through it all!

Here's what God said to His people in Isaiah: "Do not fear, for I have redeemed you; I have summoned you by name; you are mine. When you pass through the waters, I will be with you; and when you pass through the rivers, they will not sweep over you. . . . For I am the LORD your God" (Isaiah 43:1-3, NIV). Maybe you are walking through a rushing river right now. Have faith that God will never let you go under. He is with you through it all. Lift up your head and know that He is God. Don't allow fear from the enemy to control you.

God's got this—and He's got you.

A YOUNG GIRL NAMED MARY

She was a young peasant girl, engaged to be married. Then one day an angel showed up. Nearly every time an angel shows up in the Bible, people are frightened. Why? Probably because angels are not the cute little cherubs that we see in paintings or sculptures. They are warriors and servants of God. Somewhere along the way (probably with some help from the enemy), we developed the notion that angels are chubby, childlike creatures who wear diapers, float around, and play harps. This could not be further from the truth. Angels are terrifying and powerful.

I believe that how we view angels can influence how we live spiritually. If we view angels as weak and docile, then many times our faith is weak and docile. If we view angels as strong and mighty, then our faith is strong and mighty because our God is greater! Angels are warriors, and God uses them to protect us. This should give us boldness and confidence to live our lives for His glory.

After greeting Mary, the angel quickly said, "Do not be

afraid" (see Luke 1:30), because he knew that Mary was alarmed by his message and also likely by his appearance. I love that this is usually the first thing angels say: "Do not be afraid." (Maybe you need to hear these same words today!)

The angel proceeded to tell Mary what God was going to do in her life. Mary would be the bearer of the Messiah— God's own Son! Jesus was born of a woman (He was fully man so that He might identify with the struggles we go through), but He was also born of the Holy Spirit (He was fully God so that He would have the power to do something about our struggles). Mary, the angel said, would become pregnant by God's Spirit and give birth to Jesus.

This was a defining moment in human history, but think about what must have been going through Mary's mind. Just moments prior she was probably pondering her life. She had wedding plans, after all. How would her fiancé, Joseph, respond when she revealed her pregnancy? Would he believe that the child was indeed the Son of God? Perhaps the wedding had already been announced. How was her life about to change? (Keep in mind that, back in Mary's day, if a woman was found to have committed adultery, she would be stoned to death!)

This defining moment in human history meant that Mary might have to put her life on the line for God and for the child inside her. This was no small commitment. How much fear was running through this young girl's mind? Would Mary trust this angel? Would Mary trust God? Would she choose fear or faith? Would she welcome God's call to live an extraordinary life?

While we're pondering these questions, Mary proceeded to give the perfect response. "I am the Lord's servant," she answered. "May your word to me be fulfilled" (Luke 1:38, NIV). In essence, Mary was saying, "My life is not my own. I want to do what God wants me to do." Mary didn't have all the answers. She didn't know how Joseph would respond. But she trusted God nonetheless. In her defining moment, Mary chose faith over fear.

We will all have moments when we are faced with choosing faith over fear. There will be times when you, like Mary, don't have all the answers—moments when you'll need to decide whether or not you will trust God with your life. Will you respond, "I am the Lord's servant"? It's my prayer that we all make a commitment to choose faith over fear. This is where life gets exciting!

What if Mary had responded differently? We will never know, because she embraced the call to live her extraordinary life. She chose faith over fear, and God used her to help change the world.

DON'T GET STUCK

Trapeze artists are awesome to watch. They swing from one trapeze to the other, flying through the air and often trusting someone else to catch them. Every time I watch them perform, I think about that moment when they have to let go.

After all, if they don't let go—say, if fear grips them—then they will keep swinging in the air. Eventually their momentum will slow until they finally come to rest, hanging there above the crowd.

Stuck.

That is what fear does—it causes people to get stuck in life. Stuck in a job they don't like. Stuck in an unhealthy relationship. Stuck financially. Stuck spiritually. And once they're stuck, they just hang there.

Some people continue hanging on for dear life because they are afraid to let go and trust God. They don't believe that God will catch them. But God never wants anyone to just hang there. In fact, if God is calling you to let go of something—a mistake, a relationship, a troubled past—then He is always there to catch you. God is probably reaching out to you before you even realize that you're stuck.

The Bible says it this way: "For we live by faith, not by sight" (2 Corinthians 5:7, NIV). This means that we don't have to know the future—we just have to know that God is calling us to let go of the past. Mary didn't have all the answers, but she knew that God did. As you press into knowing Jesus, He will make things in your life clearer. He will give you wisdom regarding the decisions you need to make. Yet there will still come a time when you'll have to let go of your fears and trust that God will catch you.

Fear keeps many people from trusting God. From making a personal commitment to Jesus. From attending a church or joining a community of believers. From getting baptized.

From serving, giving, or going on a mission trip. And then those same people complain that they feel unfulfilled. That they don't have any deep relationships or meaning in their lives. That they are afraid.

I say that it's time to let go of fear and step out in faith. This is how we come alive. Every person who lives an extraordinary life has come to the point of letting go. And they did! They stepped out in faith and trusted God—and God caught them. They experienced the thrill of swinging on the trapeze of life and discovering the joy that comes when you are reaching out to God's waiting grasp.

The stronger you grow in your faith, the more opportunities you'll have to let go. Do you have worries from the past that keep you paralyzed? Let go. Is a sense of inadequacy keeping you stuck? Let go. Do you want to serve, but fear is gripping you tightly? Let go. Do you need to forgive someone, but every time you get close, you find yourself stuck again? Let go. Maybe you're simply afraid to give up control.

Let. Go!

Let go and trust that God can catch you. Trust that God can provide for you. Trust that God has your best interests in mind. An extraordinary life is lived by faith, not fear.

NEVER GIVE UP

One of my historical heroes is a man named William Wilberforce. He grew up in a wealthy British family during the late 1700s and was elected to a parliamentary seat at age twenty-one. Despite his relative youth, William soon gained a reputation as one of Britain's most eloquent political speechmakers.

At age twenty-five, William experienced what he called "the great change"—he surrendered all to Jesus Christ. He remained in politics, at least in part through the influence of a former slave trader named John Newton who had repented of his slave-trading past and become a minister and abolitionist. (John Newton is probably best known for writing several popular hymns, including "Amazing Grace.")

William's newfound faith was the beginning of his transformation from ordinary to extraordinary. He could have remained complacent and enjoyed an easy life in Parliament, but he knew there had to be more to life. He had God's business to attend to.

William felt God's call on his life, so he devoted himself to caring for the least, the last, and the lost. He famously wrote his life's mission in his journal: "God Almighty has set before me two great objects: the suppression of the slave trade and the reformation of manners." The first of these two seemed impossible. At the time there were hundreds of thousands of slaves throughout the British Empire. The British economy was built on slaves. How could he ever suppress this evil, yet deeply ingrained, institution?

William knew that God would have to change men's hearts. If the people of Britain would open their eyes to what is true, what is moral, what is right, and what is dignified, he thought, then maybe they would someday address the moral atrocity of slavery. William began working tirelessly to end slavery in Britain. It seemed impossible, but William had moved from the ordinary to the extraordinary, and that's where God does much of His greatest work.

William initiated his plan in 1787, and by 1789 he began introducing measures in Parliament to abolish the slave trade—yet every time they were soundly defeated. He received threats from business owners, and his efforts impacted his finances and his comfortable, affluent life. But he didn't give up. For nearly twenty years William continued introducing bills in Parliament, and for nearly twenty years they were voted down. Imagine all those years of defeat and wondering if things would ever change.

On February 23, 1807, the House of Commons debated yet another bill proposed by William Wilberforce, but this time a breakthrough was near. This time the bill finally passed by a margin of 283 votes to 16. The House erupted, chanting Wilberforce's name, and the British slave trade was ended at last!

Think about the lives that were saved and how the world was changed because William never gave up. He didn't settle for the ordinary life but lived the life God had for him. He continued to advocate for the complete abolition of slavery, but that effort took another twenty-six years. William died just one month before the House of Lords passed the Slavery Abolition Act.

William Wilberforce fulfilled the purpose God had for him. Will you fulfill God's purpose for your life? Maybe God has not called you to take on a detestable practice like the slave trade, but He has called each of us to do something for His glory.

Don't settle for the ordinary when God is calling you to so much more. Ask Him for direction, and when God makes clear His plan for your life, invest all your time, energy, and effort into fulfilling that purpose. You will be glad you did.

Whenever you feel like giving up—and you likely will at some point—remember how long it took William Wilberforce. Don't ever give up when God has called you to do something significant for His Kingdom. It might seem small to you, but God's purposes are never insignificant. So keep talking to others about Jesus. Keep taking your family to church. Keep serving those in need. Keep investing in the things of God. God's timing is not our timing, but God is always at work. And when God is at work, you're sure to see Him work wonders.

11
the BEST
iS Still
to COME

Hope springs eternal.
ALEXANDER POPE

I GREW UP LOVING BASKETBALL, and I will never forget going to a game featuring the NBA's San Antonio Spurs. It was incredible to watch these guys play. As a kid I was astounded by the way these athletes could run, jump, and dunk. Watching the Chicago Bulls' Michael Jordan fly through the air, shoot, and handle the ball was amazing. I think he is the greatest basketball player of all time! (I know, I know—many NBA fans think LeBron James is also a contender.)

It is well documented that in Michael Jordan's sophomore year of high school, he didn't make the school's varsity basketball team. So how did he react? He could have gone home and sulked. He could have quit basketball. He could have given up and thought, *I'm just not good enough.* But he didn't. Instead, he let it motivate him. He had a dream of playing in the NBA, and he would not be deterred. That setback prompted him to work harder than ever.

We can remain frustrated by what a coach, a parent, or a boss said to us in the past. We can even allow it to define us, as many people do. But we need to move beyond the past and determine to fulfill the dreams God has placed in our hearts.

I know people who, even ten, fifteen, or twenty years later, continue to let a past rejection define them. A past rejection from a boy or girl keeps them from asking anyone else out on a date. A past rejection from a boss keeps them from going after a new job. A past rejection from a parent keeps them from becoming a parent themselves. But we need to move on from the past in order to move on from ordinary.

As you've been reading this book, what has God put on your heart? What God-given dreams are welling up inside you? It probably doesn't involve playing in the NBA, but maybe it's having a godly marriage. Maybe it's raising godly children and transforming your family legacy. Maybe it's becoming a teacher, a foster parent, or a volunteer leader in your church. Maybe it's starting a business or ministry. Maybe it's becoming the man or woman God created you to be.

We all have areas in our lives that need refining. God is calling you to confront the sin or insecurities in your past and to move forward in grace and freedom. He's calling you to live your extraordinary life.

SEE SETBACKS AS A NEW START

We all experience setbacks. Your setbacks probably had little to do with high school basketball, but maybe you lost your job, went through a divorce, or filed for bankruptcy. Maybe all three. Some setbacks are small, some are big—but there is no setback that's too big for God to use in your life.

My nephew Luke grew up playing baseball, and he was extremely good at it. During his senior year of high school, Luke was one of the best pitchers in the state of Kentucky. Baseball was his life. He had big dreams of earning a scholarship to play baseball in college. His dreams included maybe even pitching in the major leagues someday. But all that changed when Luke was pitching in the state championship game and blew out his pitching arm.

It was a devastating injury. That summer Luke had Tommy John surgery (a procedure performed to repair a torn ligament inside the elbow). It was a long, difficult recovery, and all his scholarship offers disappeared because of his injury. But Luke never gave up on his dream. He followed the doctor's orders. He rested and waited. He eventually began working out again.

After a year of rehabilitation, Luke was able to start throwing again. Since the major universities had pulled away, Luke played for a junior college. He kept getting stronger. Luke was determined.

Two years later Luke was back and pitching better than ever. Once again he was being scouted by major colleges.

He went with the University of Louisville and became one of their best pitchers. Despite arm surgery, COVID-19, and other setbacks, Luke never gave up on his dream. And now he was finally living it.

But there was still something missing in Luke's life. Baseball was his everything, but baseball doesn't offer grace and peace and love. There was a God-shaped hole in Luke's life, and he was starting to figure that out. He had achieved his dream, but inside he knew there had to be more. During his junior season, while he was pitching against the University of Miami, Luke tweaked his arm. It wasn't the same sort of blowout he'd suffered before, but he could tell something wasn't right—and so could the coaches. They pulled him from the game, and his season was over.

Luke was heartbroken. Everything in his life up to that point had centered on baseball. He didn't know if he would ever pitch again. He felt lost. That's when a friend—also a baseball player—called Luke and invited him to church. Luke didn't normally attend church, but he didn't have anything else to do and thought it would be nice to see his friend again.

Luke went to church with his friend, and God began to work in his heart. Luke was given a Bible, and he began to read it. He started in the Gospel of John and found that he couldn't stop. He read all night. He went back to that church, and his friend gave him a book about the Christian life called *What Is the Gospel?* Luke read that book too.

Luke later described what God did in his life when he put his story down on paper to share with the church:

> Through the process of reading John and that book, I finally noticed how much I had fallen short of God's glory, and I understood there was nothing I could do to be made right with God except for trusting in Christ through faith and repentance. I realized how temporary baseball really was and that it could be snatched away from me anytime. However, God is eternal and lasts forever, which is something that I now knew could never be taken away from me. One night I got down on my knees and committed my life to Jesus. I asked Jesus to forgive my sins, and I dedicated the rest of my life to Him.

Luke told our family this great news, and we all celebrated with him. He invited us to his baptism, along with the entire baseball team! Before he was baptized, Luke shared his testimony in front of the church. "Baseball used to be my god," he said, "but now Jesus is the Lord of my life." It was a holy, life-impacting moment, and it showed that the best was still to come for Luke.

Today, Luke is healthy and pitching again. He doesn't know whether he will ever make it to the major leagues, but that is no longer his only goal. His goals now include living his life for the glory of his great God. He longs to be a professional baseball player, if that is what God desires, and to use his platform to further God's Kingdom. But now he also longs to be a godly husband and father one day. He longs to fulfill God's plans for his life, whatever they might be. There is a joy and a peace in Luke now that we never saw before. God has done something wonderful in him.

Did you notice how God turned Luke's personal setbacks into the start of something remarkable in his life? After Luke was injured, not only was he determined to get healthy again, but he also took the time to examine his heart and the direction of his life. This is what setbacks can do for all of us. You don't need to be a top-level athlete like Michael Jordan or Luke—any sort of setback can be a setup for what comes next.

Not every setback in your life will be the start of something new, but let's not discount the possibility. The future is often very different from what we imagine, and when God is involved, it is frequently even better. You see, God's light shines the brightest in the darkest night. We sometimes find the greatest hope and strength in the most challenging of times.

THE LIFE OF TIM BURKE

Six years ago, Tim was told by his doctor, "You are terminal."

Tim's response? "Well, aren't we all terminal?"

That's Tim all right—full of life and making the most

of every moment. Six years ago, Tim was diagnosed with prostate cancer and given five years to live. Maybe. He was a successful mortgage banker living in Southern California with a wonderful wife and two great kids. Tim had been a Christ-follower for a long time, but that moment was the catalyst that drew him even deeper into his faith. From then on, Tim endeavored to use every moment he was given for the glory of God.

I became friends with Tim about four years ago when he, his wife, Colleen, and their twins, Nolan and Irelan, moved to Franklin, Tennessee.

"We thought God was bringing us to Vanderbilt for the oncology department," Tim said, "but really, God was bringing us to Rolling Hills for our faith and community. God knew what we would go through and how much we would need a church community around us."

Tim became an instant leader in the church, and his passion for Christ was contagious. He and his family joined a community group and faithfully attended Sunday morning worship. Their kids participated in student ministry, and Tim and Colleen even toured Israel with a group from our church. The last four years of Tim's life were difficult, filled with chemotherapy treatments, yet he continued to grow in spiritual depth and maturity.

Eventually a doctor told Tim, "You have ninety days to live. You'd better get your affairs in order."

Once again Tim responded in typical Tim fashion: "Shouldn't I always have my affairs in order?"

Can you imagine how you'd react if you knew you only had ninety days to live? What would you do? As Tim reminded us, we should always have our affairs in order.

When the doctor finally put a number on Tim's remaining days, Tim immediately thought of those in his life who did not know Jesus. He sent out more than fifty copies of Lee Strobel's book *The Case for Christ* to people whose faith he wasn't sure about. He shared on Facebook how God had not caused his cancer but had allowed him to have cancer in order to use him for His glory. Tim was bold in his postings, encouraging people to make the most of their lives *right now*—to invest in things that matter and to not settle for the temporary things of this world.

I was particularly struck by what Tim did for his kids. He began making videos for those special moments he knew he would miss. His two children were in high school, so he recorded a video for them to watch when they graduated. He made another one for the first day of college. Yet another was filled with wisdom and advice for their first major job interview. He finally recorded one for his daughter to view on her wedding day, since he would no longer be there to walk her down the aisle. Yes, Tim made sure that his affairs were in order.

At our church we schedule our sermon series a couple of years in advance. For the spring of that year, we had already made plans for a series called "Finish Well" about the apostle Paul's last letter. When Paul wrote to Timothy, he knew he was going to die. Paul had been imprisoned in Rome for his faith, and so he wrote a letter (2 Timothy) to his spiritual "son" in the faith. Historians think that Timothy didn't receive the letter until after Paul's death.

As the time to launch the series approached, I asked Tim if he would be willing to record some videos for the church about how to "finish well." He did, and how God used those videos still resonates today.

I will always cherish my time with Tim. I remember going to his house to bring him cookies or a chocolate shake, and we usually ended up sitting together and talking about the deeper matters of life. I never once heard Tim complain. I never heard him be mad at God. We talked a lot about heaven. We prayed a lot and cried a lot too. His wife, Colleen, was amazing in her care for Tim, especially during his last days. Tim's only regret was that Colleen had been there for him in the toughest time of his life, but he would not be there for her in her toughest time (after he passed).

On Saturday, May 19, 2018, Tim Burke went home to be with Jesus. He truly "finished well." He lived the extraordinary life God had for him. He lived a life of love. Our work, our possessions, even our accomplishments—all these shall pass. But our love will remain. Tim loved Jesus with all his heart. Tim loved his wife and provided for her, even after he was gone. Tim loved his kids, and today they are amazing adults. Tim loved his church and every person God put in his life.

I never heard Tim say a bad word about anyone. Even after he got sick, Tim didn't spend a minute blaming God or anyone else. He was the most positive, joy-filled, full-of-life person I have ever met. He truly made the most of his days, and so many of us are better for it.

I believe that Tim heard those words we all long to hear: "Well done, good and faithful servant" (Matthew 25:21). He met Jesus face-to-face. He never lost his joy or his humor, even in the midst of suffering. He used the moments God gave him on this earth to further His Kingdom. Tim was larger than life, even in death. He inspired us all. For Tim, the best has truly come.

Before his death in 1899, evangelist Dwight L. Moody famously said: "Some day you will read in the papers that D. L. Moody, of East Northfield, is dead. Don't you believe a word of it! At that moment I shall be more alive than I am now."

My friend Tim is more alive today than ever before.

THE HOPE OF HEAVEN

Picture in your mind the most beautiful view you have ever seen. Maybe it was in the mountains. Maybe it was at the beach. Maybe you've been to a lake house where the sunrise was magnificent. Maybe it was a particular sunset you will never forget. Wherever it was for you, now imagine something a hundred times more beautiful . . . and lasting forever. It's hard to imagine, isn't it? And even this description doesn't do justice to what heaven will be like.

So many people seem to live for the moment, but deep

down we all have a longing for more. This world is not all there is. We all know this on some level. Virtually every major culture and civilization throughout history has participated in some form of worship. Why is that? Could it be that we know, intuitively, that we were made for something more? Not only is there more to come, but this current world is just the introduction.

The real story is what happens next.

It's easy to get caught up in this world because we know so little about the next. It's hard to imagine what we cannot see. Yet Jesus often taught about eternity. God wants us to know what is to come. Heaven will be amazing! Glorious. Ideal. Perfect.

As we read in Genesis 1:1, "In the beginning, God . . ." God is the author and creator of the entire world. And in the beginning, God created the heavens and the earth. He created the sky and the seas. He created the trees, plants, and animals. And He created people—male and female— who were in right relationship with God and each other. Everything was perfect, at least for a time. (For two chapters, to be specific.) Then sin entered in. The humans essentially said, "God, we don't want to do it Your way, we want to do it ours." And we've mostly been doing the same thing ever since.

But even as humankind sinned, God set into motion a plan to redeem us. He made a covenant with His people, then sent His only Son to die on a cross for the forgiveness of our sins. And He did this for all of us. As Romans 10:13

says, "Everyone who calls on the name of the Lord will be saved." God is drawing all people to Himself, and those who respond will spend eternity with Him.

At the very end of the Bible, in the book of Revelation, we read, "Then I saw a new heaven and a new earth, for the first heaven and the first earth had passed away, and the sea was no more" (Revelation 21:1). Just four verses later, the Lord says, "Behold, I am making all things new" (Revelation 21:5).

When sin entered the Garden, everything changed. But now, in Revelation, we read that God will once again make everything new and right. Jesus will return and establish a new heaven and a new earth (see Revelation 21:1). When Jesus came the first time, He came in humility—conceived of the Holy Spirit and born of a woman in Bethlehem. When Jesus comes the second time, He will come in all His power and glory. He will put an end to pain. An end to sorrow. He will make all things new and right.

Imagine a world without sin. Imagine people truly loving God and loving each other. No more bitterness or anger. No more pain or suffering. No more trying to do better than anyone else. Imagine everyone united in Christ. Racism will be replaced by genuine love for one another—everyone equal in Christ. Imagine only love, grace, joy, and eternal peace. I can hardly dream of it, but I know the day is coming. I can't wait!

If you have committed your life to Jesus Christ, then when your life ends, you will go to heaven. Jesus has already atoned for your sins. As Jesus said to the thief who was crucified right next to Him, "Truly, I say to you, today you will be with me in paradise" (Luke 23:43). Did you catch that? Jesus said *today*.

We will pass from life to life. From earth to paradise. Heaven is paradise. It is the best of all places. Nothing will be damaged by sin or pollution. Nothing will be ruined by greed or lust. We will have only perfect relationships in a perfect environment. We will be with the Lord forever. God will wipe away every tear from our eyes. No more pain. No more suffering. No more death (see Revelation 21:4). To use Jesus' word: *paradise*.

Some people cannot wrap their heads around spending eternity with God. Some might wonder, *Won't we get bored?* I can't imagine that!

After all, there is no concept of time in paradise. We love our Apple watches, our smartphones, and "maximizing our time." But heaven is not defined by time; it's defined by God. We won't get bored, because we'll be fully alive.

My dad is already there, and I can't wait to see him again. He went home to heaven a few years ago, and I miss him dearly. Maybe a parent or another loved one of yours is already there. Maybe a best friend or even a child. You miss them right now, but you will have eternity together.

Heaven is a celebration—a celebration of God's presence, goodness, and grace. The Bible speaks about the "marriage supper of the Lamb" (see Revelation 19:6-10), where the union between Jesus and His church is celebrated. Imagine the best wedding you've ever been to, and now multiply that times a number too large to comprehend. The joy and celebration will be off the charts. It will be an event like no other.

If you have committed your life to Christ, then get ready for the greatest celebration in all eternity. Best of all, think about being in the presence of your loving heavenly Father forever! You'll be fully known and fully accepted, with no more worries about what someone else thinks. No more guilt. No more stress. No more insecurities. You'll be surrounded completely by love. And you'll know it. You'll know God's presence surrounding you, holding you close. For those who know Christ, this is all still to come!

When Christ-followers die, we often say they've "gone home." That's because heaven is our home. Our eternal home. Think about what it's like to be at home when everything is going right. No dysfunction, no drama—just peace, joy, and love. We enjoy the laughter and the comfort of the familiar—it feels like being under a warm blanket by a beautiful fireplace, surrounded by people we love and who love us. When things are right, home is where you are truly *you*.

And in heaven, things are *always* right. It's the perfect home.

As Jesus said in John 14:2, "I go to prepare a place for you." A *place*. Yes, heaven is a physical place. Jesus is preparing an incredible place for us. Heaven is far more than we can ever dream or imagine.

There are a few things you should keep in mind about heaven. You won't need to tell anyone about Jesus because everyone there will already know Him. You won't need to forgive anyone because everyone there will have already been forgiven. You won't need to feed the hungry or take care of the sick because everyone there will be full, healthy, and happy. That's why we should do those things here and now! When you see needs around you, help meet them. Tell the people you know—and the people you meet—about Jesus and the place He has prepared for us!

Hope is powerful. When we are looking forward to something, when we have hope about the future, then we can endure almost anything. We can better make it through the workday when we are looking forward to a vacation. In the same way, we can better make it through the challenges of life when we are looking forward to heaven.

Recognizing the depth of God's love for you and putting your hopes in things to come will prompt you to live differently. Those little problems in life won't seem so upsetting, because your hope is not found in this world. You won't always have to be right or first, because this earth is not your eternal home. Don't worry if things don't go the way you want in life, because this is not your final destination. You are only here temporarily. This life is but a mist—a vapor (see James 4:14). It's nothing compared with the eternity that is to come.

FINISHING WELL

Even if you've never read the Bible, you've probably heard about Moses. Moses was the servant God used to bring the children of Israel out of slavery in Egypt, through the wilderness, and to the Promised Land. Moses met with God on a mountain, presented to the people God's Ten Commandments, and oversaw the building of God's tabernacle. He was an incredible servant of God, and he saw God do miracles. Moses truly lived an extraordinary life.

What's really encouraging is that God used Moses in spite of his flaws. Moses accomplished incredible things for the glory of God, yet he still had to face his fears and overcome them. When God called to Moses through a burning bush (see Exodus 3)—asking him to return to Egypt and instruct Pharaoh to let God's people go—Moses made excuses and tried to get out of it.

Can you imagine God speaking to you through a blazing bush that never burns up, yet you still avoid His commands? Maybe God has called you to something and you have not done it. Maybe God has called you to be the spiritual leader in your home, to join a church, or to fulfill your purpose, but you still haven't done it. Why not begin now? For starters, you can allow God to speak to you through this book. It doesn't matter if you've said no to God before; make today the day you trust Him and say *yes*. You'll be glad you did.

Even though Moses led God's people for many years, he was not allowed to enter the Promised Land himself. Because he had disobeyed God at a critical moment after letting his anger get the best of him, he had to face God's consequences. Yet Moses learned from his mistake, and so can we.

When we come to the end of Deuteronomy, God tells Moses that he is about to die. Yet instead of being bitter, Moses looks to make everyone around him better. Moses wants to finish well. He instructs the people to remember God's law and challenges them to live for God and to love Him with all their hearts. Moses blesses the people (instead of griping about the problems they caused him) and appoints Joshua to lead them into the Promised Land. Moses modeled the goodness and grace of God. God had been faithful in Moses' life, so he trusted Him in his death.

HOW ABOUT YOU?

Moses is a great example for us. We're not ready to truly live until we are ready to die. Many (most?) people are afraid of death, but death is essentially a passage from this life to eternal life. Death is not something to fear, but rather something to prepare for and embrace. It's a motivation to get our affairs in order. One way we do this is by having a will. Wills help us take care of our families and others. We also do this with insurance—life insurance to provide for others after we are gone from this earth. But most of all, we provide for others by pouring ourselves into those who will still be around after we are gone.

When I was growing up, my father and I went camping with other dads and sons. We had a great time skipping rocks, looking for snakes and frogs, fishing, hiking, and staring up at the stars. We set up our tents and cooked over a big fire in the middle of our campsite. Toasting s'mores was always a highlight, and the talks around the campfire solidified the memories. When it came time to pack up, my dad would always say, "Leave it better than you found it." I knew what he meant: not only to take down the tents and put out the fires, but also to pick up the trash and make the campsite nice for whoever came and used it next.

Our responsibility in life is to leave things better than we found them. Maybe your family legacy needs some repair. Maybe some negative traits have been in your family for generations. Alcoholism? Addiction? Divorce? Anger? You could be the one to stop it, to change it. You could be the one to help transform your family tree. To leave it better than you found it. To make things better for the generations to come.

We should also try to leave our schools and our communities better than we found them. We should leave our workplaces and even our country better than we found them. Recognizing that we won't be around forever helps change the way we approach life. It's not about satisfying ourselves, but rather about investing in others and leaving a legacy of faith. This is how we can impact the world around us. We can't take anything with us, so let's invest in things that will last long after we've moved on.

Begin today with living for a higher calling—God's calling. The rest of your life can be the best of your life. Embrace the life that God has for you. Embrace His hope. In this life and in the life to come, God has greater plans for you than you can ever imagine! And, like Tim Burke, get your affairs in order! Time is fleeting, so share the love of Jesus with your corner of the world.

CONCLUSION

Live Your *Extraordinary Life*

You are never too old
to set another goal or
to dream a new dream.

LES BROWN

MY FAMILY GOT TO KNOW TV personality Kathie Lee Gifford when she moved to Franklin, Tennessee. We were out to dinner one night when I asked Kathie Lee if she would share some advice with my daughters. She immediately agreed.

"First," she said, "wake up every morning and put God first. Start your day with God, and live your day for Him. Second, live your passion. Pursue the desires God put in your heart. He made you in your mother's womb, and He put desires in you. Live out your passion. Finally, forgive immediately. In life, hurt people hurt people. There will be people who hurt you along the way. Don't be consumed with bitterness. Forgive—just like Jesus forgave."

I was impressed with her response, but more so because she lives out her own advice. Kathie Lee has had many ups and downs as a public figure. She experienced many joys and struggles in her marriage, and she now lives as a widow. Yet her joy in the Lord is her strength.

After forty years in New York, Kathie Lee has seen it all. She didn't lack for much growing up, but she also never dreamed of all the places God would take her. At age eleven she watched a movie produced by Billy Graham's ministry, and it changed her life forever. She committed her life to Jesus Christ and began to pursue the passions He put in her heart. Her entire family committed their lives to Jesus as well.

How appropriate that God saved Kathie Lee in a movie theater, for God would use her for His glory on stage and screen and through song. Kathie cohosted *Live! with Regis and Kathie Lee* for fifteen years, where she helped change the face of television—especially for women in broadcasting. After *Live!* she went on to cohost NBC's *Today* show with Hoda Kotb for eleven years. In total, she has been nominated for eleven Daytime Emmy Awards, winning one in 2019—the same year she left *Today*.

"It's not that I wanted to leave the *Today* show," she told *USA Today* in 2019. "I just had to leave if I wanted to actually fulfill lifetime dreams I have that I'm running out of time for."

Kathie Lee was talking about her *childhood* dreams.

"I've wanted to be in writing and producing and starring in movies since I was a small girl," she continued, "when I wrote a letter to Walt Disney and said, 'I want to make movies with you.'"

While Kathie Lee has starred on Broadway, written musicals, and received a star on the Hollywood Walk of Fame, she knows that some of her best days are still ahead—even in her seventies! And despite the heartache of losing her husband of twenty-nine years, Pro Football Hall of Famer Frank Gifford, Kathie Lee knew that his passing was not the end of the story. She gazed upon her husband's body lovingly, but she did not grieve like those who have no hope (see 1 Thessalonians 4:13). Frank was now home in heaven, where Kathie Lee knows she will also be one day. But until that glorious time, she wants to live every day fully for Jesus.

Kathie Lee chooses not to live in the past. She is focused on how God can use her in the present and the future. Her joy is contagious and inspiring, and she personifies so much of what this book is about. She lives with passion for God, working to make a difference in the lives of others. She is truly living her extraordinary life.

What about you? What dreams and passions has God put inside you that you've pushed aside? Don't miss out on what God has for you. Dream big. Pray hard. Make the Lord first in your life, and watch Him lead you. He opens doors in your life, but walking through those doors is up to you.

Moses was already eighty years old when God called him to go free an entire nation of slaves from their Egyptian masters. By God's grace he led the people of Israel through a desert and to the Promised Land.

Josiah, whom we discussed in chapter 7, was only eight years old when he became king, but he trusted in God's Scriptures and reformed his nation.

Saul (also known as Paul) was around thirty years old when Jesus met him on a road and changed his life forever. He became an apostle and took the Good News to places around the known world.

John was nearly one hundred years old when God gave him a revelation of heaven that still inspires us today.

And then there is you. Whatever age you are, God is calling you.

If you are a follower of Christ, understand that you will spend eternity in the same place as the heroes of the Bible, the individuals I've mentioned in this book, and (hopefully) many of your family members and friends. I want you to have your own stories to share. Stories of what God did in and through your life, stories of being bold and trusting God even when it seemed like the odds against you were overwhelming. With Jesus comes faith and trust. Scripture tells us that Jesus came so that we could "have life and have it abundantly" (John 10:10).

Are you living life to the full? Why or why not? It's time to put your fears aside and dare to dream. If you fall along the way, remember the words of Proverbs 24:16: "The righteous falls seven times and rises again." In his classic devotional *My Utmost for His Highest*, Oswald Chambers put it this way: "A Christian worker has to learn how to be God's man or woman of great worth and excellence in the midst of a multitude of meager and worthless things. . . . All of God's people are ordinary people who have been made extraordinary by the purpose He has given them."

Rest in the promises of God. You are extraordinary because of the life God has for you. Your eternity is secure because you believe in Jesus Christ. This world is not all there is. Death is simply a journey from life to eternal life. The hope of Christ is the hope we need. We will live truly extraordinary lives in heaven, but by God's call and His grace, He has made it possible for us to start living extraordinary lives now.

WILL YOU START TODAY?

Yes, I said *now*. Make the decision today to put Christ first and reach your full potential. Remember that it's a no-lose proposition. There is nothing you can do to make God love you any more, and there is nothing you can do to make God love you any less.

Here are some things I've learned from spending time with the inspiring people in this book—people like Kelly Minter, Mike Fisher, Kathie Lee Gifford, and all the others who are living their extraordinary lives. I refer to these things as the "Five Ps":

- **Personal**—All these people have a personal relationship with God through Jesus Christ. Not their parents' faith or their culture's faith, but their own personal faith. All the people in this book are Christ-followers. Every one of them is a work in progress, but they have all made personal commitments to follow Jesus. This is where their faith stories begin and their extraordinary journeys continue.

- **Positive**—All the people I've mentioned are not just positive, they are a joy to be around. And they remain positive people even in difficult circumstances. They understand that negativity will destroy you. Hang around negative people enough, and you will become negative. Since God is with you and He is for you, be positive about your life and your future. Consider the words that come from your mouth; speak life and not death. Encourage yourself with God's Word, and be an encouragement to others.

- **Purpose**—The people in this book have a life purpose that's bigger than their circumstances. Stop lamenting what you don't have, and focus on what you do have. For example, if you live in the United States and you have a job, a car, and a home, then you are far better off than many other people around the world. You have incredible opportunities and potential. Make the most of them.

- **Power**—The people in this book recognize the power of God. He gives us the power to change. If you have committed your life to Jesus Christ, then God's power is at work in you—the same power that raised Jesus from the dead dwells in you (see Romans 8:11). We all have so much for which to be thankful. Don't spend your time blaming others, or even yourself, for where you're at. Forgive quickly and move forward. Don't let your circumstances define you, and don't let your past define you. God has the power to *redefine* you. Move forward in Christ.

- **Potential**—The people in this book acted on their God-given potential to keep moving forward. You have not arrived, but you are progressing. We are all a work in progress, but we won't keep progressing unless we continue to act on our potential. Keep going. Don't get stuck. Trust that God has the best plan for you, and take that next right step toward the life you were created to live!

THE SECRET

The apostle Paul wrote, "I have learned the secret . . ." (Philippians 4:12). What? There is some secret to life? You better believe it! The secret to life is what everyone wants yet money can't buy. The secret to life is what the whole world longs for and every religion promotes. People living ordinary lives wonder whether such a thing really exists.

The answer is that it does exist. Furthermore, it is available to all.

Paul explained, "I have learned in whatever situation I am to be content. I know how to be brought low, and I know how to abound. In any and every circumstance, I have learned the secret of facing plenty and hunger, abundance and need. I can do all things through him who strengthens me" (Philippians 4:11-13). Imagine that. Paul's secret was . . . contentment.

Everybody wants to be *content*. People spend untold millions in search of contentment. *If I could just take a vacation to some beautiful, exotic destination,* the thinking goes, *then I would finally be able to relax and be content. If I could just have a spa day, then I would have no stress and be content. If I could just have more money, more stuff, more* . . . simply fill in the blank with whatever you think will bring you contentment. People even take this attitude toward religion. *If I just do enough right things, then maybe God will be content with me. If I meditate long enough, then maybe I will reach a higher state of contentment. Maybe I will be reincarnated as something better. Maybe I can "become one" with the universe.*

But the truth is that Christianity is not about religion. Christianity is about a *relationship*. You can have a relationship with God, Himself, through His Son, Jesus Christ. This is why Paul was saying, in essence, "I have discovered the secret! The secret is Jesus! I have learned to be content because I can do all things through Him who gives me strength."

True contentment comes when we completely yield our lives to God—when we decide to love Him with all our heart, soul, mind, and strength. This is how we find peace and fulfillment. And once we do, we can start living extraordinary lives in the power and love of Jesus. We don't have to worry about failure because Jesus has already triumphed on our behalf. We can be bold and confident. We can encourage others because we are not worried about them somehow "getting ahead" of us.

We can have victory in life and joy in the journey. Our circumstances won't define us, because our God is greater. He has already overcome for us.

One of my favorite passages in the Bible is Ephesians 3:20-21: "Now to him who is able to do immeasurably more than all we ask or imagine, according to his power that is at work within us, to him be glory in the church and in Christ Jesus throughout all generations, for ever and ever! Amen" (NIV).

Our God is able to take care of us in every situation we face, whether we're well-fed or hungry. Paul experienced both, and so do we. We all experience physical hunger at times, and that's part of life. There are good seasons and difficult seasons. Yet our God is able. Moreover, He is able to do "immeasurably more than all we ask or imagine."

Think about that—whatever your dreams are, He is able to do more. He is able to provide in immeasurable ways "according to His power that is at work within us." The same power that raised Jesus from the grave is the power that dwells in you through Jesus. This means that if God can use that power to raise Jesus, then He can restore a dead marriage, a dead attitude, and even a dead dream in you.

So keep dreaming. Don't worry about what others are doing or where others are in life. You be you. Fulfill God's plan for your life. Don't be bitter; instead, be constantly working to bless those around you. Live your life in the strength God has given you through Jesus. This is the "secret" to life, and it's how you can live extraordinarily.

SOLOMON'S CONCLUSION

The Bible tells us that Solomon asked God for great wisdom and that God granted Solomon's request. Solomon was not only extremely wise, but he was also extremely wealthy. Keep in mind, however, that you can have plenty of wisdom and still not use it in the right way. Solomon knew the right things to do, but he later chose to live for himself. Even though he got off to a great start—having a godly father, receiving a significant inheritance, building God's temple—he eventually drifted away from God and lived to please himself.

This is what happens with a lot of people. Most people don't turn their backs on God intentionally. They don't think, *God, I'm tired of You and Your ways. I am going to live for myself.* They just slowly drift away. They stop going to church, they stop serving and helping others, and they start living for themselves. They pursue the things of this world instead of the things of God.

That's what happened with Solomon. He desired wealth and pleasure. He desired the things of this world more than the things of God. He used his wisdom, money, position, and opportunities to live a self-centered, pleasure-seeking life. He began to worship pagan gods—violating the first of the Ten Commandments—in order to please the women in his life.

Finally, after all the parties, power, and pleasure, Solomon came to the end of his life. He reflected on all the things he had built, all the money he had spent, and every pleasure he had pursued. Then he wrote this in Ecclesiastes 12:13-14: "Fear God and keep his commandments, for this is the whole duty of man. For God will bring every deed into judgment, with every secret thing, whether good or evil."

It took a lifetime, but Solomon finally recognized what was really important. After drifting away from God and worshiping pagan idols, after all his pleasure seeking and all the riches he had spent, Solomon came back to say, "Trust God and do it His way." We don't need the wisdom of Solomon to spot the truth in these words.

Solomon looked back on his life with regret. He had the opportunity to live his extraordinary life, yet he blew it. He went the way of the world instead of the way of God. Finally, at the end of his life, he realized his mistakes and tried to encourage everyone who came after him.

"Fear God and keep his commandments."

Don't miss Solomon's message: Fear God. (In this case *fear* means to demonstrate awe, reverence, and respect—to put God first in your life and to live for Him.) Solomon was encouraging you, and everyone who read his words, to live for an audience of one—the Lord—rather than worry about what other people think of you. Solomon told us that "God will bring every deed into judgment." That is what God does.

At the end of Solomon's life, not only had he drifted away from God, but the entire nation of Israel was drifting away with him. As the leader goes, so go the people. God judged Solomon, and after he died, his entire nation was split in two—the northern kingdom of Israel and the southern kingdom of Judah. All because Solomon had disobeyed God and chosen to live a self-centered life.

Your obedience to God can have influence far beyond just you. Living your life for God can also make a difference in your church, workplace, community, and marriage (or future marriage), impacting your children, your grandchildren, and the generations to come. Conversely, your disobedience to God can have a lasting impact on you and those around you. (For example, ask the family members of someone who has had an affair and left his or her spouse. Just one self-centered decision can devastate untold others.) Living your extraordinary life is not simply about you. It's more important than you could ever imagine.

NO REGRETS

The apostle Paul wrote in Ephesians, "I pray that the perception of your mind may be enlightened so you may know what is the hope of His calling, what are the glorious riches of His inheritance among the saints, and what is the immeasurable greatness of His power to us who believe, according to the working of His vast strength" (Ephesians 1:18-19, HCSB). If we truly believe that God is with us and for us, then we should also believe that He gives us the power we need to remain faithful.

We don't have to constantly atone for our past mistakes. We are forgiven. Completely forgiven. We don't have to live in constant fear of messing up, because our God is the One who redeems and restores. We also don't have to fear tomorrow. It might be a cliché, but it's true—while we don't know what tomorrow holds, we do know Who holds tomorrow. Our hearts have been enlightened with the truth that we are *His* holy people. God is sovereign, both over our lives and over the world.

Contrast the apostle Paul (also called Saul) with Solomon. Whereas Solomon had a great start, Paul did not. In fact, when we first read about Saul in the Bible, he was persecuting the church. I mean, this guy hunted down Christians! He was right there when Stephen, one of the early Christians, was killed for his faith in Jesus. Then Saul headed to Damascus to persecute more Christ-followers and put them in jail.

Jesus intercepted Saul on the road to Damascus. Jesus asked him, "Saul, Saul, why are you persecuting me?" (Acts 9:4). This is how closely Jesus identifies Himself with His church. A direct encounter with Jesus radically changed Saul's life forever.

Saul began to live his extraordinary life. He used all his knowledge, wealth, and opportunities to help plant churches in the name of Jesus. He was a completely new man. He wrote to the church in Philippi, "But whatever gain I had, I counted as loss for the sake of Christ. Indeed, I count everything as loss because of the surpassing worth of knowing Christ Jesus my Lord" (Philippians 3:7-8). Paul's life—once devoted to hunting down Christians—was now filled with joy, peace, and purpose. The impact of his decision to live an extraordinary life, a life fully for God, extended far beyond himself and influenced countless generations for the glory of God!

Unlike Solomon, who came to the end of his life filled with regret, Paul came to the end of his life filled with joy, peace, and fulfillment. The consequences of Solomon's self-centeredness and worldly desires tore a nation apart, while the love and ministry of Paul changed the world by bringing hope and redemption in Christ that continues to this day.

The love of Jesus flowed through Paul, and our world has never been the same. Paul wrote at the end of his life, "I have fought the good fight, I have finished the race, I have kept the faith. Henceforth there is laid up for me the crown of righteousness, which the Lord, the righteous judge, will award to me on that day, and not only to me but also to all who have loved his appearing" (2 Timothy 4:7-8).

Paul lived without regrets. I pray that each of us can say the same when we come to the end of our lives. That we lived out our days for the glory of our great God. That we embraced our extraordinary life.

Not only does God have a call for your life, but He also gives you what it takes to fulfill it. You'll need to retrain your mind to pay attention when He speaks to your heart. You'll need to learn to shut out the lies or hurtful words spoken by the enemy, or by inconsiderate people, or even by mistaken people with good intentions. How many times must Satan have whispered to the apostle Paul, *You remember what you did? You killed Christians! God can't use you.* But Paul moved beyond his past. Paul listened to his God and not to his enemy.

Living an extraordinary life means following the Lord's leading rather than the world's or even your own will. Surrendering your will to His purposes is one of the best feelings in the world. Push back your fears and plow forward with God. Focus on His positive words of forgiveness and grace for both you and your family. Contemplate God's Word throughout the day to remind yourself of His truths.

God wants to, and is able to, accomplish great things through you—if you only believe and follow His lead. He might have you wait for a season, but there is an extraordinary life that awaits you, because He is an extraordinary God.

William Carey (known as "the father of modern missions" and one of the founders of the Baptist Missionary Society) famously said, "Expect great things from God. Attempt great things for God." We rarely expect God to do great things in our lives, but I want you to know He is ready and willing.

As Paul reminded us, our God "is able to do far more abundantly than all that we ask or think, according to the power at work within us" (Ephesians 3:20). This is an incredible promise and a transforming truth. What if we lived like we believe it? We could change the world.

THE POWER OF ONE

On June 5, 1989, in Beijing, a lone man in a white T-shirt stepped in front of a column of advancing tanks. In China's famous Tiananmen Square, this one man halted the Chinese military in its tracks. There is power when you step up and step out. Lives are changed in ways you never dreamed possible. There is a ripple effect across generations.

Like a rock dropped in a pond, the ripples keep spreading long after the rock enters the water. The rock is you, and the ripples are the impact of your life. When you live your extraordinary life, you can impact generations to come. Your obedience in accepting God's invitation can help change the world.

I first mentioned my friend Mary Katharine Hunt in chapter 9. For many years Mary Katharine had a good job, was making good money, and was doing good things, but she still wasn't fulfilled. Then, when she was in her early forties, she went on a life-changing mission trip to the Amazon. God invited her to join Him on a great adventure, one that would require her to leave her good job and step out in faith. He was calling Mary Katharine to help provide housing for orphans in Moldova, to take food to the hungry in the Amazon, and to teach pastors and other ministry leaders how to minister to underprivileged and underserved communities.

It was a tough decision. It would mean a pay cut and a change of lifestyle. As Mary Katharine prayed and wrestled with God, she couldn't help but think about the tremendous need and how God could use her. She finally said yes to God, and hers has been an incredible journey! (You might even call it extraordinary.) Today, Mary Katharine Hunt is the executive director of Justice & Mercy International, an organization through which she is able to impact lives around the world. Yes, Mary Katharine is truly living her extraordinary life.

I remember when God called my wife, Lisa, and me to leave where we were serving to start a new work. At the time I had a great job with a very nice salary. One day I spoke at a seminary, and one of the professors there said he had a sense that God was calling me to plant a church.

Honestly, I had never even thought about that. I came home and told Lisa about it, then we prayed together and asked God to give us clarity about whether this was what He really wanted us to do. Next, I called six friends of mine and asked them to pray with us about it. After a time of seeking the Lord, it became obvious that this was indeed the next step in our journey of following Him.

We began to prepare for launching this new church, which would become known as Rolling Hills Community Church. And we continued to pray. At last came the moment when I would need to resign from my job and move to a growing area in Middle Tennessee.

I admit that I was scared. I would be giving up a great paycheck and this amazing thing called "benefits." I struggled to see how moving into a role with no guaranteed salary and no benefits would allow me to provide for my family and to accomplish what God had for our lives.

That's when Lisa said something that changed my way of

thinking: "I don't want to look back on my life one day and think, *What could God have done?* I want to look back on my life and say, 'Look what God did!'"

I finally concluded that accepting God's call was not about being *successful,* but about being *obedient.* God had made it clear, and our faith was in Him. I focused on Philippians 4:6-7, which says, "Do not be anxious about anything, but in everything by prayer and supplication with thanksgiving let your requests be made known to God. And the peace of God, which surpasses all understanding, will guard your hearts and your minds in Christ Jesus."

Twenty years ago, we stepped out and trusted God, and life ever since has been the most amazing journey ever! I feel truly blessed beyond measure.

For all of us Christ-followers, there came a defining moment when we answered Jesus' invitation to follow Him. Then came the daily commitment—moving boldly through each day in the joy and strength of the Lord. Yes, there are challenges and struggles along the way, but when you are on a journey with God, His presence changes everything.

First God changes your life, then He changes the lives of other people through you. Living an extraordinary life begins with you. This is the power of one.

THIS IS *YOUR* TIME

Moses, David, and Solomon all had their day. Peter, James, and John had their day. Your grandparents and parents had their day. Now this is *your* day. This is *your* time. What will you do with it?

Be bold. Don't worry about messing up. Don't worry about making mistakes. Live radically. Leave it all on the field. Whether you're a mom, a dad, a leader at church, a manager, an employee, a student, or whatever, every moment counts. Every moment of every day.

Give it your best as a servant of God. Stay faithful. Live with joy and with passion. Don't waste your time comparing yourself with other people. This is your life—don't try to live like someone else. God is writing your story, so make the most of every moment.

We all get just one shot. One chance to embrace this amazing God-given life. One opportunity. Make the most of your opportunity. And while you do so, know that I am praying for you and cheering you on as you live *your* extraordinary life.

Acknowledgments

Thank you for taking the time to read this book. I hope and pray it is an encouragement to you in your spiritual journey. God has a great plan for your life, and I am thankful to be on this journey with you.

This book did not just happen. God has been working in my heart and life since before I was born. I am grateful to my parents for raising me in a great church and for the godly community I had around me in my growing-up years. I am so thankful for both my dad's and my mom's faithfulness to Jesus and their commitment to raise our family in the Lord.

By God's grace, He has blessed me with an incredible wife, Lisa. I am grateful for our marriage and for who she is as a wife, mother, and colaborer in Christ. God has blessed us with three amazing children. I love being a father, and I am so proud of Grace, Mabry, and Kate.

I want to thank Rolling Hills Community Church. I love the amazing people God has brought together in our day and generation. I am grateful to serve God alongside such godly, passionate, committed team members and friends.

Justice & Mercy International has also been a big part of my journey. I love our pastors in the Amazon, the orphaned and vulnerable children we serve in Moldova, and our JMI staff both here in Tennessee and around the world. God is doing great things at Rolling Hills and JMI—all glory to His name!

I want to give a special thank-you to Jennifer Milligan, the wonderful administrative professional who did a lot of work to help make this book happen, along with my editor, Jeff, and the entire team at Focus on the Family and Tyndale. I am so blessed to serve our great God with an incredible team of godly brothers and sisters in Christ.

Please know I am praying for you as you continue to grow in your personal relationship with our Lord Jesus Christ. To Him be glory forever and ever (Ephesians 3:20-21). Thanks again for reading and growing. Blessings on you today!

Notes

CHAPTER 2: EMBRACE GOD'S HEART

28   *What comes into our minds when we think about God is the most important thing about us*: A. W. Tozer, *The Knowledge of the Holy* (New York: HarperCollins, 1978), 1.

39   *The purpose of life is not to be happy. It's to love God . . . to have it make some difference that you have lived and lived with significance*: Tim Tebow (@TimTebow), Instagram post, May 7, 2022, https://www.instagram .com/p/CdQnF92uhnD/?hl=en.

CHAPTER 4: MAKE THE MOST OF YOUR LIFE

80   *We are not cisterns made for hoarding; we are channels made for sharing*: See Billy Graham, Facebook, April 16, 2018, https://www.facebook.com /ReverendBillyGraham/posts/we-are-not-cisterns-made-for-hoarding -we-are-channels-made-for-sharing-god-has-g/10156275127902505 /?paipv=0&eav=AfZ6Z3EFpl2kGh1GdMbYQSZaq-RZmXPrtkz7mf9 WBc7rLSdurOtcAbEW7fLmlaNXzNk&_rdr.

CHAPTER 6: CHOOSE JOY

113   *Joy, which was the small publicity of the pagan, is the gigantic secret of the Christian*: G. K. Chesterton, *Orthodoxy* (London: The Bodley Head, 1908), 296.

120   A news report about the North Carolina woman and her pet python can be found here: "Woman Protects Pet as It Swallows Her Hand," *Greensboro News & Record*, January 22, 1992, https://greensboro.com /woman-protects-pet-as-it-swallows-her-hand/article_e45510ab-5997 -541c-92ae-1e4186edac49.html.

CHAPTER 10: FAITH OVER FEAR

188   *God Almighty has set before me . . . the suppression of the slave trade and the reformation of manners*: John Pollock, *Wilberforce* (London: Constable and Company, 1977), 69.

CONCLUSION: LIVE *YOUR* EXTRAORDINARY LIFE

212   *It's not that I wanted to leave the* Today *show. . . . I've wanted to be in writing and producing*: Erin Jensen, "Kathie Lee Gifford Says 'Today' Exit Isn't Sad: 'I Certainly Won't Bawl Like a Baby,'" *USA Today*, March 29, 2019, https://www.usatoday.com/story/life/tv/2019 /03/29/today-show-exit-kathie-lee-gifford-hoda-kotb-final-show /3299811002.

214   *A Christian worker has to learn how to be God's man or woman . . . made extraordinary by the purpose He has given them*: Oswald Chambers, *My Utmost for His Highest*, October 25 entry, https://utmost.org /submitting-to-god's-purpose.

About the
Author

JEFF SIMMONS is the founder and senior pastor of Rolling Hills Community Church in Franklin, Tennessee. He loves serving where God is moving in a mighty way, and he is thankful to work with amazing people whom he loves. There's no place he would rather be!

Jeff graduated from Baylor University and Southwestern Seminary. He was a student pastor with middle school, high school, and college students for ten years in Texas and Tennessee before planting Rolling Hills more than twenty years ago. He also serves as the president of Justice & Mercy International, a nonprofit organization that exists to make justice personal for the poor, the orphaned, and the forgotten of the world.

Missions is another major passion for Jeff. From the Amazon jungle in Brazil to the sunflower fields in Moldova, one of Jeff's greatest joys is serving the lost and the least of these around the world and sharing Jesus with them.

He is the author of the books *Immeasurably More* and *Eyes on Jesus*. Jeff is a dedicated family man, and his favorite hobby is simply spending time with his wife, Lisa, and their three amazing daughters—Grace, Mabry, and Kate.

FOCUS ON THE FAMILY.

STRUGGLING WITH SERIOUS ISSUES?

You don't need to do it alone. Talk to someone – at no cost to you.

Find help here
FocusOnTheFamily.com/gethelp